MOSES IN THE FOURTH GOSPEL

STUDIES IN BIBLICAL THEOLOGY

A series of monographs designed to provide clergy and laymen with the best work in biblical scholarship both in this country and abroad.

STUDIES IN BIBLICAL THEOLOGY

MOSES IN
THE FOURTH GOSPEL

T. FRANCIS GLASSON

ALEC R. ALLENSON, INC.
635 EAST OGDEN AVENUE
NAPERVILLE, ILL.

FIRST PUBLISHED 1963
© SCM PRESS LTD 1963
PRINTED IN GREAT BRITAIN BY
W. & J. MACKAY & CO LTD, CHATHAM

As Moses lifted up the serpent in the wilderness,
even so must the Son of man be lifted up.

The Lord thy God will raise up unto thee a prophet from the midst of thee, of thy brethren,
like unto me; unto him ye shall hearken.

To my daughter Ruth

CONTENTS

Introduction   9

  I The Wilderness Imagery   15

 II Moses and Christ   20

III The Prophet   27

 IV The Serpent in the Wilderness   33

  V 'On either side one' (John 19.18)   40

 VI The Manna and the Bread of Life   45

VII The Living Water and the Rock   48

VIII The Light of the World and the Three Gifts   60

 IX 'We beheld his glory' (John 1.14)   65

  X The Farewell Discourse and Prayer   74

 XI Where Johannine = Pentateuchal   79

XII Moses and his Successor Joshua   82

XIII Christ and the Torah   86

XIV The Shepherd and the Lamb of God   95

 XV Subsidiary Points: 101
       The murmuring and attempted stoning   101
       Messiah's concealment   102
       Moses as Paraclete and Intercessor   104

XVI The Apocalypse and the Fourth Gospel   106

Index of Names   111
Index of References   113

INTRODUCTION

IT is a remarkable fact that in everyday speech we assume that this earthly life of ours corresponds to the pilgrimage of Israel through the desert. Everyone knows what is meant by crossing Jordan. No explanation is needed when a playwright chooses as a title 'Johnson over Jordan'. In particular, Negro spirituals have stressed this comparison; earthly life with its travail and burdensome wanderings is at length to be exchanged for the promised land of Canaan on the other side of the river of death, the River Jordan. To give one example, from the song 'I couldn't hear nobody pray' there are the lines,

> Chilly waters, In the Jordan,
> Crossing over, Into Canaan.

This familiar usage is not merely an apt fragment of metaphorical language; it is based upon a long Christian tradition which reaches back to the New Testament itself and which has been worked out in a whole series of comparisons and correspondences. All the main events of Israel's story, from the bondage in Egypt to the conquests of Joshua, found their counterparts in Christian experience. When we sing the hymn, 'Guide me, O Thou great Jehovah', with its references to the wilderness features (the manna, the water from the rock, the guiding pillar of fire), we are perpetuating an interpretation which has a very long and enthralling history.

Incidentally Charles Wesley followed a different interpretation of the symbolism; Canaan stood not only for the blessed life after death, but also for the life of perfect love which could be enjoyed here and now, 'the Canaan of Thy perfect love'. Scriptural warrant is claimed for this in Hebrews 4, where the promised rest is available as a present experience. For Christian thought generally, however, Jordan has stood for the narrow stream of death; and for the purpose of the present study Charles Wesley's interesting variation does not come into account. On either interpretation it was important to notice that Moses (the Law) could not lead the people into Canaan; only Joshua (Jesus) could do that. Wesley is not, of course, alone in his interpretation. In its introduction to the book of Joshua the Scofield Bible says, 'In a spiritual sense the book of Joshua is the Ephesians of the Old Testament. "The heavenly" of Ephesians is to the Christian what Canaan was to the Israelite—a place of conflict, and therefore not a type of heaven, but also a place of victory and blessing through divine power.'[1]

In the New Testament reference is made again and again to the wilderness wanderings as a type of the Christian life. In recent years increasing attention has been paid to the importance (for the understanding of the New Testament generally) of seeing the Messianic hope in terms of a new Exodus and of recognizing the Messiah as a second Moses. In the following pages it is hoped to show that this approach is one of the keys to the understanding of the Fourth Gospel. Admittedly it is only one of several, but it is an important one.

It was over thirty years ago that I read an expository volume on John 1–12 by F. B. Meyer entitled *The Life and Light of Men* (1891). Meyer, a Baptist minister, was a well-known preacher in his day and at one time he was closely associated with D. L. Moody. His numerous books on the Bible, beautifully written, were mainly devotional in character and did not set out to make new contributions of a scholarly kind; nevertheless they were the result of close study, thorough reading and genuine insight. This particular book pointed out in reference to John 6–8 that three factors of the wilderness experience here reappeared in Christian dress. In chapter 6 instead of the manna we have Christ as the true bread coming down from heaven; in chapter 7 he offers the living water corresponding to the streams from the rock which Moses smote; and in chapter 8 instead of the fiery pillar we have Christ as the Light of the World in following whom men walk no longer in darkness. About the same time I was studying Westcott's commentary on John, where the same point is made. Meyer very likely derived this exposition from Westcott, and he was always ready

[1] In some early baptismal rites milk and honey were given to the candidate as a sign that he had entered the promised land (so O. Hardman, *History of Christian Worship*, 1937, p. 27). The Non-Jurors sought to revive this use of milk and honey. Origen in his *Homilies on Joshua* uses the crossing of Jordan as a type of baptism; but normally the crossing of the Red Sea was reserved for this.

to acknowledge his debt to the great commentators of the time. This interpretation of John 6–8 seemed to me to be so obvious that I have seldom referred to this section of John since without recalling it. Although Westcott pointed out the importance of the wilderness experience generally for the understanding of John, this has not always been remembered in subsequent work on the Gospel. Nevertheless it has, as we shall see, an unexpectedly wide relevance.

The word 'Moses' is sometimes used to cover the five books of the Torah, as in the phrase 'Moses and the prophets', and I have at times referred to this wider connexion. In the main, however, we shall be concerned with Moses as a person and with the events associated with his leadership from Egypt to the borders of the promised land. The term 'John' is used both for the Evangelist and his book, without making any assumptions on the question of authorship.

One matter of importance must be mentioned at this point. Most of the Rabbinic evidence which it is customary to adduce, in connexions such as our present study, was actually written down after the first Christian century. It is therefore possible for anyone to say that this or that piece of evidence is inadmissible on account of its late date, i.e. the date of its written form. Several factors indicate that this is not a fatal difficulty, though the objection is useful in calling attention to the need for care and discrimination. The Mishnah itself, one of the most important of all Rabbinic sources, was not written down until about AD 200. But it is generally agreed that it contains much material of a far earlier date. Quite often the names of the Rabbis are attached to their sayings; this enables us to say with some confidence that certain ideas were extant in the time when the New Testament was being written. The Tosephta is usually regarded as roughly contemporary with the Mishnah.

Most importance is naturally to be attached to the earlier rather than the later Rabbinic writings. The Targums contain a good deal of teaching which can safely be regarded as extant in New Testament times. Among the commentaries the Mekhilta (on Exodus), Siphra (on Leviticus) and Siphre (on Numbers and Deuteronomy) are of special value. With regard to the collection of Midrashim known as Midrash Rabbah, those dealing with

Genesis and Leviticus are older than the rest; Exodus R.[1] and Deuteronomy R. are the latest in date. Even in a late Midrash we occasionally find sayings attributed to very early authorities, and in these cases opinion about their genuineness may be divided. To give an example, in Deuteronomy R. a saying about Moses returning to the world with Elijah is attributed to Johanan ben Zakkai, who lived in the first century AD. Some authorities, like Billerbeck, say that this saying may be no earlier than the year 900, when the complete work was written; others contend that there is no reason to regard it as other than a genuine saying of Johanan. D. Daube, in his valuable book *The New Testament and Rabbinic Judaism* (1956), gives another interesting example. He shows that the phrase 'Moses' seat' cannot be found in Rabbinic sources until some centuries after New Testament times; but the fact that it occurs in Matt. 23.2 is pretty good evidence that it was in use among first-century Jews and the lack of earlier attestation is a mere accident.[2]

However, the material with which we are mainly concerned holds together with a certain consistency; and the way in which it illuminates and explains factors in the New Testament that are otherwise mysterious provides some justification for the view that it represents a tradition already in existence in New Testament times. It is generally recognized that the Jewish material presented in such works as Strack-Billerbeck and the Kittel Word-Book is of enormous value and importance in interpreting the New Testament writings, in spite of the fact that much of it was recorded after the first Christian century.[3]

The standard commentaries on St John are referred to in the following pages by the surnames of their authors, and it is to be understood that Barrett, Hoskyns, Lagrange, Westcott and so on, when accompanied by no book title, refer to the commentaries on St John which they have written (C. K. Barrett, *The Gospel according to St John*, 1955; J. H. Bernard, *International Critical Commentary*, 2 vols.,

---

[1] Exodus R. means the commentary on Exodus in the Midrash Rabbah, and so with the other books in this collection.

[2] He calls this 'a striking illustration of the fact that an institution or idea may be early even though mentioned only by the later Rabbis' (p. 246).

[3] Cf. J. W. Doeve, *Jewish Hermeneutics in the Synoptic Gospels and Acts*, 1953, especially ch. 2, 'The Serviceableness of the Rabbinic Data for the Examination of the New Testament'.

1928; E. Hoskyns, *The Fourth Gospel*, 1940; M.-J. Lagrange, *Evangile selon S. Jean*, 1925; R. H. Lightfoot, *St John's Gospel: a Commentary*, ed. C. F. Evans, 1956; A. Loisy, *Le quatrième Evangile*, 1903, 2nd ed. 1921; B. F. Westcott, *The Gospel according to St John*, 1880). Similarly the work by C. H. Dodd, *The Interpretation of the Fourth Gospel*, 1953, is cited as 'Dodd'.

The abbreviation S.B. stands for *Kommentar zum Neuen Testament*, by H. L. Strack and P. Billerbeck; and *TWNT* for *Theologisches Wörterbuch zum Neuen Testament* (ed. G. Kittel and G. Friedrich).

Quotations from the Mishnah are given mostly according to the English translation of H. Danby, *The Mishnah* (1933), Clarendon Press. Quotations from Philo have been taken from the translation of F. H. Colson and G. H. Whitaker in the Loeb Classical Library (Heinemann). Those from the Midrash Rabbah have usually been taken from the Soncino Press edition of 1939, *Midrash Rabbah*, 10 vols., edited by H. Freedman and M. Simon.

I

THE WILDERNESS IMAGERY

BEFORE we look closely at the Fourth Gospel it will be a help to consider the more general Christian and Jewish background. Among New Testament references to the wilderness wanderings as a type of the Christian life, one of the most important passages is I Cor. 10:

For I would not, brethren, have you ignorant, how that our fathers were all under the cloud, and all passed through the sea; and were all baptized unto Moses in the cloud and in the sea; and did all eat the same spiritual meat; and did all drink the same spiritual drink: for they drank of a spiritual rock that followed them: and the rock was Christ. (1–4.)

According to verse 6 'in these things they became figures of us' (RV margin). Elsewhere it is made clear that the deliverance from Egypt corresponds to the salvation wrought by Christ; he is himself the Passover lamb, as in I Cor. 5.7 f. and I Peter 1.18 f. When on the mount of Transfiguration reference is made to the decease which he was about to accomplish at Jerusalem, the word used for decease is *exodos*, and there may be a hint here that the Old Testament story is being repeated on a higher plane, particularly as Moses appears in the context. The Christian counterpart of the crossing of the Red Sea is the Resurrection of Christ: Heb. 13.20 (reflecting Isa. 63.11). We may compare Neale's Easter hymn, 'The foe behind, the deep before', in which the deliverance from Pharaoh and the Resurrection of Christ are jointly celebrated. The very title New Testament means New Covenant, and this replaces the covenant at Sinai, both being ratified by the blood of the covenant (Ex. 24.8 and Mark 14.24).

This usage goes back to Jewish eschatology and is rooted in the Old Testament itself. For the people of Israel, the Exodus was not only the outstanding deliverance of the past and the beginning of the national history, but it became a symbol and pledge of the expected deliverance of the future. The Messianic time was thus in part modelled upon the Exodus and its sequel; and as we shall see later, Moses as deliverer foreshadowed the Messiah. The Jewish scholar J. Klausner in his *Messianic Idea in Israel* (1956) says that the traditions about 'the saviour of Israel' who brought out his people from the first captivity 'comprise the authentic embryo from which the Messianic idea of necessity developed' (p. 18). As Westcott put it in a comment on John 1.29, 'The deliverance from Egypt was the most conspicuous symbol of the Messianic deliverance'; he refers in illustration of this important principle to Ezek. 20.33 ff.:

I will bring you out from the peoples . . . with a mighty hand . . . and I will bring you into the wilderness of the peoples, and there will I plead with you face to face. Like as I pleaded with your fathers in the wilderness of the land of Egypt, so will I plead with you, saith the Lord God.

This passage reminds us of the earlier words of Hosea 2.14 f.:

Therefore, behold, I will allure her, and bring her into the wilderness, and speak comfortably unto her . . . and she shall make answer there, as in the day when she came up out of the land of Egypt.

Again it is said in Isa. 10.24–26 that if the Assyrian oppressor smites 'after the manner of Egypt', the Lord of hosts will intervene on Israel's behalf and will lift up his rod over the sea 'after the manner of Egypt'. The Assyrian menace is dealt with in similar terms in Isa. 11.15 f. We find the same imagery in Micah 7.15: 'As in the days of thy coming forth out of the land of Egypt will I shew unto him marvellous things.' Deutero-Isaiah is specially rich in such passages.[1] The return of the exiles would be like the journey from Egypt to the promised land. But the prophet makes it plain that he did not think there was to be a detailed repetition of all the features of the Exodus; he was concerned with the main thought of divine deliverance. This is made clear in Isa. 52.12, 'For ye shall not go out in haste, neither shall ye go by flight: for the Lord will go before you; and the God of Israel will be your rear-

---

[1] J. Fischer in 'Das Problem des neuen Exodus in Js 40–55' (*Theologische Quartalschrift* 110 [1929], pp. 111–30) gives the following passages from Isaiah as illustrating the new Exodus: 40.3–5; 41.17–20; 42.16; 43.1 f.; 43.19–21; 48.20 f.; 49.9b–13; 51.9 f.; 52.11 f.; 55.12 f.

ward.' The absence of haste is in contrast with the conditions of the original Passover, when the bread was unleavened and they stood staff in hand. The latter part of the verse, however, shows that the divine presence and protection could be depended on as before (Ex. 14.19). The main idea was that God was unchangeable, and since he had delivered his people from the house of bondage at the beginning of their national history, so in the new captivity in the east he could be depended on to repeat his mighty acts.

While the prophets were speaking of their immediate situation, all these forecasts and assurances gave rise to a significant element in the Messianic hope which is of great importance for both Christian and Jewish thought. A full and comprehensive survey of this subject has been given by Dr Willi Wiebe in his Göttingen Dissertation (unfortunately unpublished), *Die Wüstenzeit als Typus des messianischen Heilszeit*, to which I am indebted at this point. In this he not only gives an account of the Old Testament material and its sequel in later Jewish writings, but also shows the importance of this approach for almost every part of the New Testament.[1]

It is of importance for our present subject that specific features of the wilderness life were expected to reappear. Once again there would be streams in the desert. Thus Deutero-Isaiah says of the new Exodus from Babylon, 'And they thirsted not when he led them through the deserts: he caused the waters to flow out of the rock for them; he clave the rock also, and the waters gushed out' (48.21; cf. 49.10). So in Isa. 43.19 there is the promise, 'I will even make a way in the wilderness, and rivers in the desert.' Other features connected with the first deliverance are to appear again, e.g. the pillar of cloud and fire (Isa. 4.5). The covenant made at Sinai has its counterpart in the New Covenant of Jer. 31.31 ff.

This background enables us to understand why it was that deliverance was frequently associated with the wilderness: Isa.

---

[1] Cf. also J. Daniélou, *Sacramentum Futuri* (Paris, 1950), especially Livre iv, ch. 1, 'La typologie de l'Exode dans l'Ancien et le Nouveau Testament': pp. 131 ff.; J. Guillet, 'Le thème de la Marche au désert dans l' Ancien et le Nouveau Testament', *Recherches de Science Religieuse* 36 (1949), pp. 161–81; J. Marsh, *Fulness of Time* (1952), ch. 4. Dr Ulrich Mauser has more recently dealt with the question of the significance of the wilderness in the Old Testament in ch. 11 of his book *Christ in the Wilderness* (1963, SBT 39).

40.3, 'Prepare ye in the wilderness the way of the Lord.' It is true that here the wilderness is that which lies between Babylon and Palestine, just as the original wilderness lay between Egypt and Palestine; nevertheless even after the return from the exile the future Messianic deliverance was still looked for in the desert. Mention is made of this in the Dead Sea Scrolls, and it partly explains why the members of the Qumran sect went into the desert and settled by the wady Qumran. In the New Testament we find John the Baptist carrying out his work in the desert. Some of the first-century rebels mentioned by Josephus were similarly connected with the wilderness (cf. Matt. 24.26). Theudas led his followers to the Jordan with a view to dividing the waters (*Antiquities* 20.97–99); other unnamed leaders led the people 'into the desert' (*Jewish War* 2.259). The anonymous Egyptian of Acts 21.38 led 4,000 Assassins 'into the desert'; cf. *Jewish War* 2.261.

Since special attention has been drawn to Deutero-Isaiah in the foregoing, it may be mentioned in closing this chapter that some scholars have suggested that the Servant of the Lord is presented as a second Moses[1] who is to lead the people in the new Exodus. This is stressed by A. Bentzen in his *King and Messiah*:[2]

The Servant is sometimes compared with Moses or Joshua, especially in the so-called second song (49.5–6, 8–12) . . . The Servant of the Lord is described as a new Moses or Joshua, leader of the new Exodus and of a new allotment of the land to the tribes. It must, therefore, be considered very probable that the Ebed Yahweh in the scheme of Deutero-Isaiah played the role of the 'new Moses'—'Moses redivívus', by which I do not mean a reincarnate or returned Moses (p. 66).

S. Mowinckel in *He that Cometh* (1956) disagrees with this; yet he is willing to allow that 'certain traits from the figure of Moses may have been present to the mind of the poet, when he painted his picture of the Servant' (p. 228). Again on p. 232:

. . . some scholars have seen in the Servant a new Moses. To later ages, Moses was the prophet *par excellence*, the pattern for all prophets. An important element in the tradition about Moses is his constant

---

[1] Cf. Delitzsch on Isa. 53 (*Biblical Commentary on the Prophecies of Isaiah* [trans. Denney], II, p. 313): 'according to Isaiah 42, 49 and 50, the Servant of Jehovah is first of all a prophet, and as the one who proclaims a new law, as the Mediator of a new covenant, he is another Moses.'

[2] 1955: translated from *Messias—Moses Redivivus—Menschensohn*.

intercession for the sinful people. He is even ready to die, in order to appease the wrath of Yahweh against the people; and the punishment for their sins falls on him as well. It is quite possible that the memory of these ideas helped to form the portrait of the Servant in the mind of the poet-prophet.

Claude Chavasse (*Theology* 54 [1951], pp. 289 ff.) has shown, in some detail, grounds for the possibility 'that Deutero-Isaiah may have taken the title My Servant, and certain elements in his character, though not the whole portrait, from Moses'.

This is of great interest in connexion with the ministry of our Lord. Those who believe that Jesus saw in his own ministry the fulfilment of the Servant prophecies (cf. Luke 22.37) will find here support for the view that he regarded himself as a second Moses. But for our present purpose it is unnecessary to reach a decision on this matter[1] and we may leave it as an open possibility. Of greater importance is the more direct Jewish expectation of a second Moses, and to this we now turn.

[1] The work of Morna Hooker, *Jesus and the Servant* (London, 1959), must be seriously faced.

II

MOSES AND CHRIST

CLOSELY connected with the Exodus and wilderness complex, as foreshadowing the Messianic deliverance, is the figure of Moses as foreshadowing the Messiah himself. The Jews envisaged a parallelism between Moses and the Messiah probably before the Christian era.[1] There is ample evidence in Rabbinic writings that Moses was called the first deliverer and the Messiah the second deliverer; and while this evidence is mostly later than New Testament times as far as its written character is concerned, there can be little doubt that this particular form of Messianic hope originated in the pre-Christian period.

It should be noted that this is quite apart from any Messianic use of Deut. 18.15, the promise of a prophet like unto Moses. The Samaritans, it is true, used Deut. 18.15 as a Messianic proof-text and even attached it to their version of the Decalogue. With them the Messiah was given the title *Ta'eb* and he was to be a teacher. In John 4.25, where the Samaritan woman describes the Messiah as one who should 'teach us all things', we have an accurate reflection of this view.[2] But it is a mistake to say that the Jews had no doctrine of a second Moses at this period on the ground that they, unlike the Samaritans, do not quote Deut. 18. The important point is that the coming deliverance was to be a repetition of the deliverance from Egypt, and *therefore* there would be a second deliverer (the Messiah) comparable to the first (Moses).

In this connexion a Rabbinic passage, to which there are many parallels, may be quoted from the Midrash Ecclesiastes R. on Eccles. 1.9:

R. Berekiah said in the name of R. Isaac: As the first redeemer was, so

[1] See especially the article Μωυσῆς in *TWNT* by J. Jeremias (IV, pp. 852–78).
[2] J. Bowman in a valuable paper read to the New Testament Society in 1955 traced a number of points of contact between the Fourth Gospel and Samaritan theology. Cf. *Bulletin of John Rylands Library* 40 (1958), pp. 298–308.

shall the latter Redeemer be. What is stated of the former redeemer?
And Moses took his wife and his sons, and set them upon an ass (Ex.
4.20). Similarly will it be with the latter Redeemer, as it is stated,
Lowly and riding upon an ass (Zech. 9.9). As the former redeemer
caused manna to descend, as it is stated, Behold, I will cause to rain
bread from heaven for you (Ex. 16.4), so will the latter Redeemer
cause manna to descend, as it is stated, May he be as a rich cornfield
in the land (Ps. 72.16). As the former redeemer made a well to rise,[1]
so will the latter Redeemer bring up water, as it is stated, And a fountain shall come forth of the house of the Lord, and shall water the
valley of Shittim (Joel 4.18 [EVV, 3.18]).

In spite of the date of this particular passage,[2] which is similar to
a considerable number, there can be little doubt that such ideas
were 'in the air' in the time of our Lord and earlier. It perhaps
belonged to popular expectations rather than to definite Rabbinic
teaching at that stage (cf. *TWNT* IV, p. 866). The Messianic
pretenders mentioned by Josephus evidently saw themselves in
the light of this second Moses tradition. They led their followers
into the desert, or attempted to divide the waters in the manner
of Moses.

The importance of this Moses/Messiah parallelism has not
always been sufficiently recognized in interpreting the New
Testament. While in these pages we are thinking mainly of the
Fourth Gospel, brief mention may be made of the fact that the
influence of this parallelism may be traced in many places elsewhere. The text of Deut. 18.15 is quoted in Acts 3.22 and 7.37;
and Stephen's speech in the latter chapter draws out at length the
similar treatment accorded to Moses and Jesus, and describes
how both were rejected by their brethren, who did not recognize
that God was offering deliverance by their hands. But quite apart
from the quotation of Deut. 18, a whole series of references springs
from the Moses/Christ argument. Thus in St Matthew the phrase
in the Nativity story, 'they are dead that sought the young child's
life' (2.20), is clearly a reflection of Ex. 4.19, where the Lord says

---

[1] The Soncino translation here given adds as a footnote at this point
'v. Num. 21.17 f.'.

[2] The date of Berekiah is *c.* AD 350 and that of Isaac *c.* 300. Evidence for
the Moses/Messiah typology may be found in the teaching of Akiba, who
flourished 90–135; see *TWNT* IV, p. 865.

to Moses, 'Go, return into Egypt; for all the men are dead which sought thy life.' The connexion is clearer in the Greek: Matt. τεθνήκασιν γὰρ οἱ ζητοῦντες τὴν ψυχὴν τοῦ παιδίου. Ex. τεθνήκασι γὰρ πάντες οἱ ζητοῦντές σου τὴν ψυχήν. There are several points of comparison in the Temptation story when considered side by side with the forty years' testing of Israel. In both there is the wilderness as the scene of temptation; the replies of Jesus all come from Deuteronomy and from passages which relate to the testing of Israel. Here in a sense Jesus is the essential Israel (as in Matt. 2.15); but the forty days and forty nights (Matt. 4.2) correspond with a period mentioned in the story of Moses (Ex. 24.18; Deut. 9.9). In Matt. 5–7 the Messiah gives a new law ('it was said of old time . . . but I say unto you') and this corresponds to Moses receiving the first law on a mountain.

Even a familiar passage such as Heb. 13.20 ('who brought again from the dead the great shepherd of the sheep' ὁ ἀναγαγὼν ἐκ νεκρῶν τὸν ποιμένα τῶν προβάτων) appears to reflect the influence of the Moses/Messiah parallelism. Westcott's note in his commentary on Hebrews is worth quoting: 'The old commentators saw rightly in the words here a reference to Isa. 63.11 LXX ποῦ ὁ ἀναβιβάσας ἐκ τῆς θαλάσσης τὸν ποιμένα τῶν προβάτων. The work of Moses was a shadow of that of Christ: the leading up of him with his people out of the sea was a shadow of Christ's ascent from the grave: the covenant with Israel a shadow of the eternal covenant.'

The Moses/Christ parallelism is in a sense a part of the wider context of the wilderness imagery, but it also merits special consideration on its own account. Before we look more particularly at the relevance of this approach to the Fourth Gospel it may be pointed out that the whole question of the Moses/Christ parallelism has never been entirely lost sight of, though its importance has been recognized more keenly in some periods than in others. Two examples from Christian art are representative of a larger number:

(*a*) In the Catacombs there are a number of pictures in which this parallelism is to be found. In several instances a representation of Moses and the rock from which the waters flowed is paired with one of Jesus raising Lazarus from the dead; e.g. Wilpert's *Roma Sotteranea* (Rome, 1903), II *Tav*. 248, where both Moses and Jesus are seen holding a rod. Here the rod has been clearly introduced into the story of Christ from the Exodus story of Moses. Again there is a picture of the wedding at Cana, in which Jesus touches the water pots with a rod; and Moses appears in one of the marginal pictures adjoining.

(*b*) In the Sistine Chapel at Rome, the wall frescoes give the story of Moses on one side and the story of Christ on the other. This shows how familiar the thought was at this period; the choice of subjects was probably fixed by Pope Sixtus IV (1471–84). The Journey of Moses corresponds to the Baptism of Christ; the Leading into the Wilderness, to the Temptation; the Passage of the Red Sea goes with the Calling of the Apostles; the Giving of the Law to the Israelites with the Giving of the Law to Christians; the Gainsaying of Korah with the Giving of the Keys to Peter; the Testimony and Death of Moses with the Last Supper; and finally the Burial of Moses (and the contest between Michael and Satan) with the Resurrection of Christ. In the time of Sixtus there was also, on the altar wall, an Assumption of the Virgin flanked by the Finding of Moses and the Birth of Christ; these are now obliterated by Michelangelo's Last Judgment.

Behind these artistic presentations there was, of course, a continuing literary tradition. The subject is repeatedly mentioned in patristic writings, though at times the sound biblical interpretation becomes interlocked with too much allegory. Eusebius in his *Demonstratio Evangelica* draws out a dozen points of comparison between Moses and Christ; they include the following. Both were legislators. Moses appointed seventy elders; Jesus seventy disciples (Luke 10.1). Moses fed the people in the wilderness; Jesus fed the crowds. The shining of Moses' face is coupled with the Transfiguration. Both fasted for forty days. 'But why need I seek further for proof that Moses and Jesus our Lord and Saviour acted in closely similar ways, since it is possible for anyone who likes to gather instances at his leisure?' (III.2).

This parallelism crops up even in the debates between Roman Catholics and Protestants. Thus Stillingfleet's *Irenicum* (seventeenth century) points out that the Romanists and others who stand for fixed and detailed forms of church government, were in the habit of arguing 'from the comparison of Christ and Moses' that as 'Moses appointed a particular form of Government for the Church under the Old Testament, therefore Christ did certainly lay down a form of Church Government for the New Testament' (p. 176).

However, the first scientific and thorough treatment of the subject in modern times was the work of A. F. Gfrörer, *Das Jahrhundert des Heils*, vol. II (1838). He discusses, in this scholarly work, the various forms of Messianic expectation in the time of Jesus, including the Davidic and those evidenced in the apocalypses; but he gives a large amount of space to the Messiah considered as a second Moses. He quotes the passage from the Midrash on Ecclesiastes which has already been given in this chapter and describes the lively joy he felt on discovering it in 1831. Even a man who is half blind, he says, can see its utmost importance for the study of the New Testament.

The importance of Gfrörer's work was fully realized by a number of scholars in the nineteenth century, but more recently disproportionate attention to the apocalyptic writings has obscured it. A century ago Westcott in his *Introduction to the Study of the Gospels* had a chapter on the Jewish doctrine of Messiah; and it is interesting to note that a paragraph on 'the Davidic type' is followed by a longer paragraph on 'the Mosaic type'. The former, he says, played a larger part in the expectations of the mass of the people;

but the image and promise of Moses moulded the expectations of some among them. These looked for a Prophet rather than for a King, though they entertained no clear conception of the scope of his teaching; and the 'likeness' of which Moses spoke led them to anticipate an outward resemblance in life rather than in work between the lawgivers of the Old and New Covenants, which attained in later times a fabulous minuteness.[1]

Here a footnote refers to Gfrörer's work.

In the following chapters it will be shown how important for the study of St John's Gospel is the Moses/Christ complex. The Prologue ought to suggest this to us, for in 1.17 we have the statement, 'The law was given through Moses; grace and truth came through Jesus Christ.' Here there is both a contrast and a comparison.[2]

[1] 8th ed., 1895, pp. 132 f.
[2] It may be pointed out here that it is not worth while making an accurate

24

The very next verse probably continues the thought. Emphasis was often laid by the Jews upon the closeness of Moses' communion with God (Deut. 34.10); there was a sense in which he was granted a vision of the divine (Ex. 33), but this was partial and incomplete, so that it still remained true that 'no man hath seen God at any time' (John 1.18). In contrast with this is the perfect knowledge and revelation of God associated with the only-begotten. The very words 'No man hath seen God at any time' remind us of the statement of Ex. 33.20, 'Thou canst not see my face; for man shall not see me and live'. (The RV Old Testament reference for John 1.18 is Ex. 33.20.) Jews in their adulation of Moses had drawn attention to him as a man of vision; as Heb. 11.27 puts it, 'He endured as seeing the invisible.' Westcott's comment on the Hebrews passage is:

The most characteristic trait in the life of Moses is that he spoke with God face to face, Ex. 33; Num. 12.7, 8. The 'vision of God' is that which distinguishes him from the other prophets.

Philo had described Moses as searching 'everywhere and into everything in his desire to see clearly and plainly him, the object of our much yearning, who alone is good'; yet he goes on to say that Moses failed to gain his object, for 'he alone by his very nature cannot be seen' (*De Mut. Nom.* 2). Again in his life of Moses, Philo describes Moses as beholding what is hidden from the sight of mortal nature (1.28).[1]

The very passage of Exodus (ch. 33) to which Jews appealed in their glorification of Moses, itself yields the stricture that 'no man shall see me and live.' So that if John 1.18 is continuing the contrast with Moses indicated in the previous verse, he is tacitly drawing attention to the fact that while Moses was a man of vision, the scriptures make it plain that he did not see God. The Son of God, however, has and communicates perfect knowledge

---

division between passages which contrast Moses and Christ and others which compare them. Every comparison involves an element of contrast, and it is taken for granted that in every respect Christ is greater than Moses (cf. Heb. 3.3). It is impossible to contrast two objects or persons unless they have much in common.

[1] That Philo described Moses as *theoptēs* (beholder of God) is doubtful; see the note on *De Mut. Nom.* 2 in Colson and Whitaker's edition (Loeb Library) which shows that the reading here is uncertain.

of God (1.18b). Cf. 6.46, 'Not that any man hath seen the Father, save he which is from God, he hath seen the Father.'

Thus at the outset of the Fourth Gospel we find the co-ordination of Moses and Christ in comparison and contrast. Mention should also be made of the Torah/Logos theme of the Prologue; for Moses is important not only as a prophet and deliverer but as the embodiment of the Law, as in the phrase 'Moses and the prophets'. Running right through the Prologue is the transference to the Logos of what had been claimed for the Torah. Fuller reference to this will be made in a later chapter.

The whole of the first chapter of St John is in a sense preparatory. When we come to the second chapter, we may find a point of contact in the first sign of Jesus at the wedding at Cana (2.1 ff.). The change of water to wine should remind the reader of the first of the plagues in Egypt, the changing of water to blood. There is a verbal echo of the Exodus story which would confirm that this was in the Evangelist's mind. Ex. 7.19 says that 'there shall be blood throughout all the land of Egypt, both in vessels of wood and in vessels of stone'; cf. John 2.6 with its reference to the 'waterpots of stone'. Some words of Archbishop Trench in his book *Notes on the Miracles* may be quoted here:

This first miracle of the New Covenant has its inner mystical meaning. The first miracle of Moses was a turning of water into blood (Ex. 7.20); and this had its fitness; for the law, which came by Moses, was a ministration of death, and working wrath (II Cor. 3.6–9). But the first miracle of Christ was a turning of water into wine, this too a meet inauguration of all which should follow, for his was a ministration of life. . . .[1]

From another angle, the waterpots, 'set there after the Jews' manner of purifying' (2.6), symbolize the religion of the Law, now replaced by the festive wine of the gospel.[2]

[1] 13th ed., 1886, pp. 121 f.
[2] The waterpots 'stand for the entire system of Jewish ceremonial observance', says C. H. Dodd, p. 299. He points out that the first sign illustrates the doctrine of John 1.17.

III

THE PROPHET

THERE are a few Johannine references to 'the prophet' which may be considered here, since these are best explained in connexion with Deut. 18.15–18. In some places the prophet is distinguished from the Messiah (1.25; 7.40 f.), and in another place apparently identified with him (6.14 f.). It is of interest that Jewish expectations concerning Moses took two forms; and that while some looked for a second deliverer, a Messiah conceived along Mosaic lines, others thought of a return of Moses as a forerunner of the Messiah.

Expectations of a new advent of Elijah are well known because of the words of Mal. 4.5 f. But other forerunners were at times mentioned also; cf. II (4) Esd. 6.26. Enoch occasionally is included here. But there is evidence that in some quarters Moses and Elijah were to be the two forerunners.[1] The Rabbinic evidence for this is very late, but there can be little doubt that it reflects a much earlier view. In Deut. R. 3.17 God says to Moses, 'By your life! as you laid down your life for them in this world, so in the time to come, when I send them Elijah the prophet, you will both come at one time.'[2] One reason for postulating a much earlier currency for this expectation is to be found in Rev. 11, where the two witnesses who herald the end are coloured respectively by characteristics of Moses and Elijah; they 'have the power to shut the heaven that it rain not' (11.6) as Elijah did (I Kings 17), and 'they have power over the waters to turn them into blood, and to smite the earth with every plague' (11.6)—this clearly reflects the ten plagues associated with Moses, particularly

---

[1] Cf. G. H. Boobyer, *St Mark and the Transfiguration Story*, 1942, pp. 69–76.
[2] This should not be discounted because of its late attestation; as I. Abrahams writes, 'Though this occurs in a late source, it is obviously of early origin, there being no reason for doubting its ascription to Johanan b. Zakkai (first century)' (*Studies in Pharisaism and the Gospels* II, 1924, p. 53).

the first of them, the turning of water into blood. The presence of Moses and Elijah at the Transfiguration is probably another reference to the tradition in question. If Jews were to raise the objection that Jesus could not be the Messiah because the two expected forerunners had not appeared,[1] the Transfiguration provided an effective reply.

In the light of all this it is interesting to find in the same context (John 1.19–25), in the questions addressed to the Baptist, references to Elijah and the (Mosaic) prophet, so that verse 25 virtually includes the Messiah and his two forerunners. It is difficult to understand why in this record John repudiates the suggestion that he is Elijah.[2]

Our immediate concern, however, is with the prophet and with the three passages where he is mentioned, 1.21; 6.14 f.; and 7.40. In the last two cases it is mooted whether Jesus himself is the prophet, and here it is clear that Moses is in mind as 6.14 follows the miracle of the loaves and is followed by a discourse on the manna, while 7.40 follows the reference to the gift of living waters, which, as we shall see, is in all probability to be connected with the Horeb incident of Ex. 17.

In two of these three cases (1.21 and 7.40) the prophet is distinguished from the Messiah. John denies he is Messiah, but is nevertheless asked as an alternative if he is the prophet. Again in 7.40 f. some in the crowd surmise that Jesus is the prophet, others that he is the Messiah.[3] But in 6.14 f. we appear to have a different

---

[1] Justin's *Dialogue with Trypho* 49 shows that this objection was made by Jews in so far as Elijah was concerned. Christians usually replied by pointing to John the Baptist, whose ministry is an essential part of all the Gospels; in Acts, too, the gospel begins not with the baptism of Jesus, but 'the baptism which John preached' (10.37; 13.24).

[2] Perhaps the point is that John is not to be regarded as the return of the historical Elijah—and this is what the Jews were expecting. That he may still be a forerunner working 'in the spirit and power of Elijah' (Luke 1.17) is not necessarily denied in John 1.21. In fact, there is evidence that the Evangelist thought of the Baptist in this way; the description of John in 5.35 as a burning and shining lamp appears to reflect the reference to Elijah in Ecclus. 48.1 ('Also there arose Elijah the prophet as fire, and his word burned like a torch'). For an alternative explanation of John 1.21 see J. A. T. Robinson's article 'Elijah, John and Jesus: an essay in detection', *New Testament Studies* 4, pp. 263–81; reprinted in *Twelve New Testament Studies* (SBT 34), 1962.

[3] J. B. Lightfoot in *Biblical Essays* (1893), writing on 'Internal evidence for the authenticity and genuineness of St John's Gospel', makes the acute

presentation; when the crowd concluded that this must be 'the prophet that should come into the world', Jesus perceived that they were about to make him a king. Here the prophet and the Messiah seem to be equated. Several explanations are possible:

(*a*) It may be that some in the crowd thought he was the prophet, and that others (unmentioned) thought he was the Messiah; verse 15 refers to this second group which we have to envisage by reading between the lines.

(*b*) Perhaps a better suggestion is that of Lagrange, who points out that 1.21 and 7.40 find their setting at Jerusalem, while 6.14 comes from an incident in Galilee. It may be that the Jews of Jerusalem, instructed by the Pharisees (and of course in 1.21 the speakers were emissaries of the Pharisees), distinguished the prophet from the Messiah, while among the Galilean populace there was a tendency to identify them.[1]

(*c*) The truth of the matter may be that since there was a certain fluidity in Jewish Messianic ideas, it is wrong to expect a consistent scheme. The apparent divergence of 6.14 f. from the other two passages could then be regarded as a true reflection of these inconsistent elements.

There can be little doubt that the Evangelist himself regards Jesus as (among other things) the true fulfilment of the hope for 'the prophet that should come into the world'.

There may be a further reference to the prophet in John. One of our oldest manuscripts, the Bodmer Papyrus II (P[66]), inserts the article before 'prophet' in the statement, 'Search, and see that out of Galilee ariseth no prophet.' With the article the translation would be, 'the prophet ariseth not from Galilee.' Incidentally this would relieve the difficulty that has often been felt about this verse; it was simply not true that there had been no Galilean prophet—Jonah was from Galilee, and the Pharisees would know this. Bultmann some years ago had conjectured that the article

---

remark that since Christian thought identified Christ and the prophet like unto Moses (Acts 3.22; 7.37) it is hardly conceivable that a Christian writer, if he were living in the second century and were calling on his imagination for facts (as extreme critics had suggested), should have divested himself so absolutely of the Christian idea.

[1] See his comments on 6.14 and 7.40; also p. cxxxiii, where the same point is made.

originally stood here and the reading of P⁶⁶ gives strong support to this conjecture. E. R. Smothers in an article on two readings of the Bodmer papyrus[1] favours the acceptance of 'the prophet' in John 7.52; and, as he shows, it suits the context well. Thus in verse 40 some suggested that Jesus was the prophet; and it was in reference to this that the Pharisees maintained that the prophet would not arise from Galilee (52).

Mention may be made at this point of a reading for Luke 7.39 which is found in the important manuscript B (and a few others—the reading is accepted by Weiss) according to which Simon the Pharisee said in himself, 'This man if he were the prophet . . .' Whether the prophet is referred to in Matt. 21.11 is uncertain, 'This is the prophet Jesus, from Nazareth of Galilee.'

There can be little doubt that the way in which Christ is presented in the Fourth Gospel is intended to indicate that he is the fulfilment of Deut. 18.15–19. This is, of course, only one element among several, but it is an important one. The words of verse 18 should be specially noted: 'and I will put my words in his mouth, and he shall speak unto them all that I shall command him.' There appear to be distinct echoes of this in John. The RV marginal references to the words just quoted from Deuteronomy ('he shall speak', etc.) are all from John: 4.25; 8.28; 12.49 f. Jesus says, 'I do nothing of myself, but as the Father taught me, I speak these things' (8.28); 'For I spake not from myself; but the Father which sent me, he hath given me a commandment, what I should say, and what I should speak . . . the things therefore which I speak, even as the Father hath said unto me, so I speak' (12.49 f.). It is rather curious that commentaries on John do not always recognize the Old Testament undercurrents of these passages. John's constant emphasis on Jesus acting in his Father's name corresponds to the prophecy 'my words which he will speak in my name' (Deut. 18.19).

The prophet was to be like unto Moses, and Moses himself is reported as saying in a passage we shall look at again later, 'Hereby ye shall know that the Lord hath sent me to do all these works for I have not done them of my own mind (LXX of myself)' (Num. 16.28), another passage which has many Johannine parallels and correspondences which can hardly be due to coincidence.

---

[1] *Harvard Theological Review* 51 (1958), pp. 109 ff.

It must be emphasized again that popular Jewish expectations of a second Moses were not all connected with Deut. 18 by any means; much more important was the idea of a second deliverer whose redeeming work would repeat the exploits of the Exodus from Egypt. In interpreting John also, the latter is the more important, though the two strands are woven together as a part of the Messianic presentation.

It is remarkable that nowhere in John is Jesus called Son of David. In fact, the only reference to David in the whole Gospel is a passage which on the surface appears to deny the Davidic origin of Jesus (7.42). This, of course, is only on the surface; it is an instance of the Johannine irony, since the writer was quite conversant with the fact that Jesus was of David's line. But nowhere is this mentioned. This is remarkable in view of the fact that 'Son of David' occurs in all the other Gospels, particularly in Matthew. That Jesus is the Christ is emphasized in John, and his kingship is repeatedly brought out, especially in the Passion narrative. The implication is that it is not a Davidic kingship[1] such as the bulk of the Jews were expecting; it is a kingdom not of this world (18.36).

It is noteworthy that Moses was sometimes described as a king in Jewish writings, and even apparently in the Old Testament (Deut. 33.5). A passage in Philo's life of Moses (I.158) is of interest here:

For he was named god and king of the whole nation, and entered, we are told, into the darkness where God was, that is into the unseen, invisible, incorporeal and archetypal essence of existing things.

It may be that in John the Mosaic strand, which is undoubtedly included in the Messianic conception, is to be connected with Christ's kingship; and that the latter should be interpreted along Mosaic, and not Davidic lines. If Moses was a king, he had little resemblance to an ordinary king. The kingship of Jesus is of the Mosaic type and is in even greater contrast with the kingdoms of this world.

The Samaritans, as we have seen earlier, interpreted their

---

[1] Cf. C. H. Dodd, 'That the Messiah is Son of David, he appears to set aside (like Mark) as at best irrelevant to the true Christian doctrine of the Messiah' (p. 228).

Messiah along prophetic lines, taking Deut. 18.15 ff. as their key passage. John 4 implies that Jesus fulfils this expectation. The woman describes the Messiah (in conformity with the Samaritan Ta'eb conception) with the words, 'he will declare unto us all things' (4.25); and Jesus replies, 'I that speak unto thee am he.'

Mention may here be made of a curious statement which is found in the Old Russian text of Josephus; a passage interpolated into the second book of the *Jewish War* contains the following in reference to Jesus: 'Everything that he performed through an invisible power he wrought by word and command. Some said, Our first lawgiver is risen from the dead, and he has displayed signs and wonders.' In the New Testament there are references to the rumours that our Lord was Elijah, Jeremiah and so on; but no hint that he was thought to be Moses raised from the dead. One wonders if this reference in the Josephus interpolation is the chance survival of a very early suggestion. The numerous indications that Jesus was considered as among other things the prophet like unto Moses would support this possibility.

IV

THE SERPENT IN THE WILDERNESS

WITH the brazen serpent of John 3.14 we come to a wilderness incident which is quite explicitly related to Christ and the Gospel: 'As Moses lifted up the serpent in the wilderness, even so must the Son of man be lifted up, that whosoever believeth may in him have eternal life.'

In the remarkable set of paintings which Tintoretto did for the Scuola of San Rocco at Venice, the ceiling panels and wall paintings in the upper hall (painted 1575–81) are of special interest, since they largely consist of incidents from the stories of Moses and Christ. The ceiling is devoted to the Old Testament, and of the three main rectangular panels the largest, in the very centre, is devoted to the Brazen Serpent. The other two depict the Gathering of Manna and Moses striking the Rock.[1] The largest and central panel thus links up with John 3, while the other two connect with John 6, which deals with the manna and its Christian counterpart, and with John 7 and its promise of living water. (The relation of this promise to the rock in the desert will be dealt with later.) Incidentally these three wilderness events are found together in Deut. 8.15–16; verse 14 refers to the Exodus from Egypt and then follow the words:

Who led thee through the great and terrible wilderness, wherein were fiery serpents and scorpions, and thirsty ground where was no water; who brought thee forth water out of the rock of flint; who fed thee in the wilderness with manna, which thy fathers knew not; that he might humble thee, and that he might prove thee, to do thee good at thy latter end.

The reference in John 3 to the brazen serpent is not just a passing

[1] The wall pictures are devoted to incidents in the life of Jesus, and there is a scheme of correspondence, no doubt worked out by the committee of the Scuola, relating these to the ceiling paintings. (Eric Newton ascribes the subject-matter to the committee and not to Tintoretto himself: *Tintoretto*, 1952, p. 124.)

allusion, and several points connected with this passage should be noticed.

1. While the word 'look' does not occur in John 3.14, it has a central place in the original narrative in Numbers 21:

And the Lord said unto Moses, Make thee a fiery serpent, and set it upon a standard: and it shall come to pass, that every one that is bitten, when he seeth it, shall live (v.8).

When we consider the importance of 'seeing' in John, we can hardly doubt that the brazen serpent reference of 3.14 should be taken into account in this connexion.[1] One of the great themes of John is the importance of beholding the Son; all the way through the Gospel this subject is referred to, and at its climax we find the words, 'They shall look on him whom they pierced' (19.37). Numbers 21 links together seeing and living: 'when he looked unto the serpent of brass, he lived' (v. 9). We may compare with this John 6.40 '. . . that every one that beholdeth the Son and believeth on him, should have eternal life'. It is remarkable that in Num. 21 it is not said that everyone who looked upon the serpent was healed, but 'when he looked . . . he lived'; and 'when he seeth it, he shall live.' Life is, of course, one of the key-words of John, and while a number of sources may be connected with this theme, the link with Num. 21 should not be overlooked; in John 3.14 f. the brazen serpent reference is explicitly linked with life: 'so must the Son of man be lifted up, that whosoever believeth may in him have eternal life.'

There is a sense in which the words of 3.14 f. could be taken as a text for the whole Gospel. The absence of the actual word 'look' is not, I think, important, since this is implied in the very reference to the serpent. The word 'see' may be found many times in the Synoptics, but where is there anything resembling the Johannine emphasis on 'seeing Jesus', on 'beholding the Son'? Consider the following:

1.14, 'we beheld his glory'; 1.29, 36, 'behold, the lamb of God'; 1.39,46, 'Come and see'; 1.50 f., 'Ye shall see the heaven opened, and the angels of God ascending and descending upon

---

[1] Cf. Dodd, pp. 306 f.

the Son of man';[1] 6.40, 'everyone that beholdeth the Son';
12.21, 'Sir, we would see Jesus'; 14.9, 'he that hath seen me
hath seen the Father'; 14.19, 'the world beholdeth me no more
but ye behold me'; 16.16, 'a little while and ye behold me no
more . . . ye shall see me'; 17.24, 'that they may behold my
glory'; 19.35, 'he that hath seen . . . hath testified'.

And in 19.37, as we have already seen, when at length the Son of
man is lifted up a special testimony is added to the story from
Zech. 12.10 which mentions not only the piercing but also the
looking. There are other examples. G. L. Phillips[2] has discussed
the various terms used for seeing in John and arranged them in a
mounting sequence; it is claimed that 'believing' supplies the
climax and final term in this series. If that were the case it would
further explain why in John 3.14 f. the word 'believeth' is found
and not 'seeth'. In any event there is a close link between seeing
and believing[3] (cf. 20.8). In some cases there is the seeing of the
eyewitness; those who come later hear his testimony and believe.
In this sense believing takes the place of seeing (cf. 19.35 and
20.29). But it is fairly clear that there are also references to a
kind of seeing which is still available to all. As B. Lindars has
written, 'To read John is an act of contemplation. . . . This act
is itself the means of appropriating the fulness of grace and
truth. . . .'[4]

2. Another point of importance is that the Brazen Serpent was
lifted up: 'as Moses *lifted up* the serpent'. This is the first occurrence of the expression in John (also found in 8.28 and 12.32, 34),
just as the same passage gives the first example of the term
'eternal life'.

In John's use of the expression there is a dual reference, or
rather it includes as in a single concept the crucifixion and the
glorification of Jesus.

[1] The reading 'from now' (at the beginning of this statement) should not
be too hurriedly dismissed; the apocalypse, the unveiling, begins with the
opening of the ministry.

[2] 'Faith and Vision in the Fourth Gospel' in *Studies in the Fourth Gospel*
(ed. F. L. Cross), 1957, pp. 83–96. Cf. E. A. Abbott, *Johannine Vocabulary*
(*Diatessarica* 5, 1905), sections 1597–1611.

[3] Discussed by O. Cullmann also in the Goguel Festschrift, *Aux sources
de la tradition chrétienne* (Neuchâtel, 1950), pp. 52 ff.

[4] 'The Fourth Gospel an act of contemplation' in *Studies in the Fourth
Gospel* (ed. F. L. Cross), pp. 23–55.

3. The term 'lift up' is often associated in the Old Testament with a standard. It is interesting to notice that the word used for the support to which the serpent was attached is the word 'standard' (Hebrew *nes*; LXX *semeion*). 'And the Lord said unto Moses, . . . set it upon a standard. . . . And Moses made a serpent of brass, and set it upon the standard' (Num. 21.8 f.). While the standard is not mentioned in John 3.14 f. it is not fanciful to suggest that in reading John, one must remember his allusiveness; one must be ready to read between the lines and to follow up hints and pointers.[1] We may therefore claim that John expected his readers to think of the standard on which the serpent was uplifted, especially since in the Old Testament the word for 'lift up' is repeatedly linked with a standard. (In Isaiah the standard or ensign is 'lifted up' in 5.26; 13.2; 11.12; 18.3; 62.10.) Thus when we dwell upon the word *nes* (standard or ensign) we soon encounter the Johannine expression 'lift up', and vice versa. The LXX does not use ὑψόω in these passages; and here I should like to say once for all that in studying John, while the LXX should never be neglected, at times it is the Hebrew Bible which leads us to essential links and connexions.

The word used in most of the Isaiah passages mentioned above for 'lift up' is *nasa'* (5.26; 13.2, etc.). And this is the word which Delitzsch uses in his Hebrew New Testament for the Johannine 'lift up' in all the passages in which it occurs. I. Salkinson and C. D. Ginsburg in their Hebrew New Testament also use *nasa'* in John 3.14 and 12.32, 34.

A further point is that the standard in the Old Testament is often associated with the gathering of the dispersed. Thus in all but one of the Isaiah passages cited above the idea of gathering is present; e.g. 11.12, 'And he shall set up an ensign for the nations, and shall assemble the outcasts of Israel, and gather together the dispersed of Judah from the four corners of the earth.' With such passages we may compare what is said of Christ lifted up on the Cross in John 12.32, 'And I, if I be lifted up from the earth, will draw all men unto myself.' Cf. 11.51 f., where

---

[1] C. K. Barrett in his article 'The Old Testament in the Fourth Gospel' (*Journal of Theological Studies* 48 [1947], pp. 155 ff.) shows that the Evangelist does not rely mainly on quotations and proof-texts, but he has, as it were, absorbed the whole of the Old Testament into his system.

Jesus is said to die that he might gather together into one the children of God that are scattered abroad.

J. B. Lightfoot thought that John 12.32 contained a reference to the prophetic image of a standard. This suggestion occurs in his comment on Ignatius' *Epistle to the Smyrnaeans* (ch. 1) where Ignatius quotes a phrase from one of Isaiah's passages concerning the erection of a standard.[1] Lightfoot points out that Jerome, quoting from an earlier commentator on Isa. 5.26, says that the standard lifted up to draw men from the ends of the earth was the Cross. It is at this point that he adds, 'There is perhaps a reference to this same prophetic image of a standard in John 12.32.'

With this association we may compare all the references to the Cross as a standard or banner, for example Fortunatus' hymn, *Vexilla regis*. The following passage from Lactantius is worth quoting, as it is surely true to John's interpretation; it also illustrates the way in which the lifting up includes both suffering and exaltation:

That also was a principal cause why God chose the Cross, because it was necessary that He should be lifted up on it, and the passion of God become known to all nations . . . so raised on high, that all nations from the whole world should meet together at once to know and worship Him. Lastly, no nation is so uncivilised, no region so remote, to which either His passion or the height of His majesty would be unknown. Therefore in His sufferings He stretched forth His hands and measured out the world, that even then He might show that a great multitude collected together out of all languages and tribes, from the rising of the sun even to his setting, was about to come under His wings and to receive on their foreheads that great and lofty sign.

(*Institutes* 4.26; W. Fletcher's trans.)

It is apposite also to refer here to the note of the famous English commentator Matthew Henry (d. 1714) on the serpent story of Num. 21.8 f., 'The word here used for a pole signifies a banner, or ensign, for Christ crucified "stands for an ensign of the people", Isa. 11.10.'

---

[1] Ignatius himself connects the standard with the resurrection of Christ, 'truly nailed up in the flesh for our sakes under Pontius Pilate that he might set up an ensign unto all the ages through his resurrection'.

4. A further point concerning John 3.14 I put forward with some hesitation as a possibility only. In the LXX of Num. 21.8 f. the word used for the standard or pole on which the brazen serpent was placed is *semeion*; this word or some cognate is regularly used for standard in the Greek Old Testament, and as we know quite definitely it also means sign or miracle and is so used in John.

Is it not possible that the Evangelist, who has so much to say about signs (*semeia*), intends us to see that the greatest sign of all is the sign of the Cross, this is the ultimately convincing wonder? Jews seek signs, but we preach Christ crucified. Here is to be seen the true power of God (I Cor. 1.22–25). We cannot speak positively on this matter, but the allusiveness of John would favour the view that he was not unaware of this further implication of the Brazen Serpent parallel.

Justin repeatedly uses the word 'sign' in connexion with the serpent; thus in his *Dialogue* (94), God 'caused the brazen serpent to be made by Moses in the wilderness and set it up for a sign by which those bitten by serpents were saved'; in the same section he refers to the Cross as 'this sign'. Again in his *First Apology* (60) he mentions the Brazen Serpent incident and then goes on to speak of 'the sign (*semeion*) of the Cross'.

It is perhaps a further support to this suggestion that there is a Rabbinic reference to the Brazen Serpent story in which the word *nes* is regarded precisely as 'miracle'. Numbers R. 19.23 (on 21.9): 'And Moses made a serpent of brass, and set it up by a miracle. He cast it into the air and it stayed there' (Soncino trans.).

It is rather remarkable that the Hebrew word *nes* means both standard and sign (or miracle), and the Greek word *semeion* has the same double connotation, it also means both standard, or something lifted up, and sign or miracle. We have seen in the previous section that although the *nes*, as standard, is not directly mentioned by John, the thought of it appears to be present and proves illuminating in connexion with other references to the lifting up of Christ. The same may be true of this other connotation, for *nes* in later Hebrew came to mean sign or miracle; this meaning does not occur in the Old Testament except that in Num. 26.10 the term is used in the clause 'they became a sign'.

But it is frequent in post-biblical Hebrew;[1] e.g. in the Hanukkah service it simply means miracle and is so translated in S. Singer's edition of the Hebrew Prayer Book (p. 274).

It may be objected that if John thought of *nes* or *semeion* in Num. 21 as standard he could not at the same time have thought of it as sign. But this objection falls to the ground when it is remembered that one of the Evangelist's characteristic usages is to take words of dual connotation and to follow both meanings.[2]

If the suggestion made in this section is valid it would support the words of C. K. Barrett, 'As in Mark, there is no miracle in the [Johannine] passion narrative. This is not because the story of Jesus ceases to have the value of revelation; in fact, the death and resurrection are the supreme *semeion*' (p. 65).[3]

[1] See Jastrow's *Dictionary of the Targumim*.

[2] Cf. O. Cullmann in *Theologische Zeitschrift* 4 (1948), pp. 360–72.

[3] Cf. Dodd, '. . . every *semeion* in the narrative points forward to the great climax' (p. 142).

Since writing the above I have read the article by J. P. Charlier, 'La notion de signe dans le IVe évangile' in *Revue des Sciences Philosophiques et Théologiques* (43 [1959], pp. 434–48), and I notice that he too draws attention to the fact that the Johannine word for sign means both evidential sign and rallying standard; in both senses, so he maintains, the Cross is the ultimate *semeion*.

V

'ON EITHER SIDE ONE' (John 19.18)

IN early Christian writings two Old Testament incidents often found together are the Brazen Serpent of Num. 21 and Moses praying at Rephidim (Ex. 17.8–16). They are found together in Barnabas 12; Justin's *Dialogue* 90 f., 94, 97, 112; Cyprian's *Exhortation to Martyrdom* 8 and *Testimonies* II.20–22.[1] In Irenaeus IV.24 they are welded together in one sentence: 'Him who, by the spreading forth of hands, did destroy Amalek, and vivify man from the wound of the serpent, by means of faith which was exercised towards Him'.

These two incidents had probably been linked together in pre-Christian times, for we find them together in Rabbinic writings. In the Mekhilta on Ex. 17.11 we have the following:[2]

It was not assuredly the uplifted hands of Moses that invigorated Israel and laid Amalek low. Israel looked at him, and, so long as he lifted up his hands, they believed on Him who had given Moses the command to act thus. God it was who did the signs and wonders on their behalf. Nor was it the serpent that killed and gave life. Israel looked, and, so long as Moses lifted up the serpent, they believed on Him who had commanded Moses to act thus. It was God who healed them.

It is remarkable that in both cases the Mekhilta mentions 'looking', though in the Bible itself this is confined to the latter story; there is no mention of looking in Ex. 17.

Again in the Mishnah, the following occurs in Rosh Ha-Shanah 3.8:

And it came to pass when Moses held up his hand that Israel prevailed, and when he let down his hand Amalek prevailed. But could the hands of Moses

[1] Even in Augustine *Contra Faustum* 12.28 f. the two are still together.
[2] As rendered in Hoskyns, p. 217, who says in introducing the quotation, 'The capacity of visible actions to awaken faith is illustrated by the restoration to life of the dying Israelites who looked at the brazen serpent which Moses had lifted up in the desert, and was recognised in the teaching of the Rabbis.'

promote the battle or hinder the battle!—it is, rather, to teach thee that such time as the Israelites directed their thoughts on high and kept their hearts in subjection to their Father in heaven, they prevailed; otherwise they suffered defeat. After the like manner thou mayest say, *Make thee a fiery serpent and set it upon a stand, and it shall come to pass that every one that is bitten when he seeth it shall live.* But could the serpent slay or the serpent keep alive:—it is, rather, to teach thee that such time as the Israelites directed their thoughts on high and kept their hearts in subjection to their Father in heaven, they were healed; otherwise they pined away (Danby's *Mishnah*, p. 192).

Since these two incidents were linked together by the Church so frequently and even as early as Barnabas's epistle (which according to some authorities may be a first-century production and may be earlier than John), we may wonder if there is any trace in John of Moses stretching out his hands, to accompany the clear reference to the Brazen Serpent,[1] especially as they appear to be already linked in Jewish thought.

Now, in reading John's account of any incident recorded in the other Gospels it is always worth while noticing any distinctive expressions, quite apart from the question of John's dependence on the Synoptics (a matter which is still being debated). Jesus was crucified between two thieves; Mark says 'one on his right hand, and one on his left' (15.27). Matt. 27.38 and Luke 23.33 have the same, except that 'the' replaces 'his'. But John puts it in this way: 'where they crucified him, and with him two others, on either side one, and Jesus in the midst' (19.18). Is it possible that the distinctive Johannine words have any connexion with the incident of Exodus 17? 'Aaron and Hur stayed up his hands, the one on the one side, and the other on the other' (17.12). Here the LXX has ἐντεῦθεν εἷς καὶ ἐντεῦθεν εἷς. John 19.18 has ἐντεῦθεν καὶ ἐντεῦθεν. If we turn this into Hebrew as Delitzsch has done in his Hebrew New Testament we have מזה אחר ומזה אחר—this is *exactly* the phrase used in Ex. 17.12. I do not suppose that Delitzsch was aware of this, and it is striking to find this agreement; but

---

[1] C. Chavasse in 'Jesus: Christ *and* Moses' (*Theology* 54, 1951) writes, 'There is one curious omission. It is strange that Moses praying on the hill overlooking Rephidim with hands held up by Aaron and Hur, and thereby causing the defeat of the forces of Amalek, is never mentioned by any New Testament writer as prefiguring the Crucifixion, when we see Jesus on the hill of Golgotha, with hands supported by nails driven in by Caiaphas and the Pharisees, and thereby defeating the forces of Satan' (p. 295).

John's Greek words are sufficiently close to the LXX to lead us
to ask if the Evangelist were consciously making a typological
allusion.

It is true that the usual phrase used by the Fathers in connexion
with this incident does not call attention to the position of Moses
between two others, but rather to the *stretching out of the hands*.
(This may lie behind the words to Peter, John 21.18, which we
shall look at in a moment.) Curiously enough Ex. 17 does not
employ the phrase, but says only that Moses lifted up his hands.
It seems probable that the use of Isa. 65.2 as a testimony referring
to the Cross[1] had encouraged the transfer of its phraseology 'I
have spread out my hands' to the Rephidim incident.

Here reference to the Sibylline Oracles 5.256–9 may be made:
'who stretched forth his hands upon the fruitful tree'. This is
usually regarded as a Christian interpolation; but Blass would
excise as Christian only the phrase 'upon the fruitful tree', re-
garding the rest as Jewish and as a reference to Moses; the words
which follow, 'who stayed the sun', are explained by the fact that
some of Joshua's exploits were transferred to Moses. H. N. Bate,
however, takes the usual view that the whole passage is Christian
and he writes, 'Christ is the second Moses (Ex. 17.12). Cf. 8.251,
ὃν Μωσῆς ἐτύπωσε προτείνας ὠλένας ἀγνάς' (i.e. whom Moses typi-
fied when he stretched forth holy arms).

T. W. Manson has discussed the joining together of the two
incidents of Moses praying at Rephidim and the Brazen Serpent,
in Jewish and Christian writings, in his article 'The Argument
from Prophecy' (*Journal of Theological Studies* 46 [1945], pp. 129 ff.).
With regard to the Fourth Gospel he admits the possibility that
the Evangelist knew of the application to the Cross of these two
incidents, even though (in Manson's view) he used only the Brazen
Serpent. But he prefers to think that the use of the Serpent
passage represents a primitive stage of the tradition, and that
Ex. 17 came into Christian use later; but both belonged to first-
century Palestinian Christianity. He thinks that the Jews then

[1] This verse of Isaiah ('I have spread out my hands all the day unto a
rebellious people') was no doubt originally used as an anti-Judaic testimony,
and it is so used by Paul in Rom. 10.21. But it was frequently used in early
Christian writings as a prophecy of the Crucifixion. Barnabas quotes it immediately after his reference to Moses at Rephidim; Justin does the same. The
latter writer quotes it five times in connexion with the Crucifixion.

rebutted the Christian use of these passages and that is why we find them conjoined in the Mekhilta and the Mishnah.

I find it difficult to accept Manson's account and to see in the Jewish references a rebuttal of Christian interpretations. To begin with, the Rabbinic treatment of the Serpent is pretty much the same as Philo's, which was certainly not anti-Christian.[1] Again, there is nothing in the Rabbinic treatment to which Christians would take exception, and no specific Christian interpretations are refuted. It seems more likely that the Rabbis had already in the pre-Christian period put together two incidents which on the surface looked somewhat magical. Later the Christians who were looking everywhere in the Old Testament for the sign of the Cross said in effect, 'We can now explain these mysterious incidents; they foreshadowed the Cross of Christ.' This is the line taken by Justin in the second century; Trypho the Jew admitted 'we cannot give a reason', when Justin asked him why Moses set up the brazen serpent for a sign, thus apparently transgressing the second commandment (ch. 94).

If the suggestion I have made earlier in this chapter is valid, then John includes both the Brazen Serpent (3.14) and, by the phraseology of 19.18, a hint of Moses praying between Aaron and Hur. If this is true we can understand why John strangely suppresses the fact mentioned by all the other Evangelists that the two crucified with Jesus were thieves; he merely says 'two others' (19.18) and again in verse 32, 'The soldiers . . . brake the legs of the first and of the other which was crucified with him.'

As we have already noticed, the idea of stretching out the hands was a recognized expression in the early Christian vocabulary for crucifixion. While it is true that the same applies to classical Greek[2] this is hardly sufficient to explain Christian usage. In classical Greek we have evidence for the verb *ekteinō*; but Christian writers did not confine themselves to this, but used a variety of

---

[1] And cf. L. Ginzberg, 'The Rabbinic explanation of the setting up of the serpent upon a pole must not be taken as an anti-Christian Haggadah, as may be seen from the fact that it was known to the author of Wisdom. It is at the same time true that in the polemic literature of the Jews in the Middle Ages the correct explanation of the serpent of brass plays an important part' (*Legends of the Jews*, vol. 6 [1928], note on vol. 3, p. 658).

[2] See quotations from Artemidorus, Epictetus, etc., in Lagrange, Bernard, Barrett, and Trench (*Miracles*, ch. 33).

expressions to convey the same meaning of stretching out or spreading forth the hands, *ekpettanumi, proteinō*, etc., and again and again we find the phrase linked with a reminiscence of Ex. 17 and often with Isa. 65.2 also. This should be borne in mind in connexion with the words of the risen Lord to Peter in John 21.18, 'When thou shalt be old, thou shalt stretch forth thy hands, and another shall gird thee, and carry thee whither thou wouldest not.' Here there is a surface meaning and a deeper meaning[1] (as in other passages of John). On the surface the words refer to an old man being helped to dress for a journey. But Christian readers would find no difficulty in discerning the hidden meaning; 'stretch forth thy hands'—i.e. on the Cross; 'gird thee' —i.e. secure thy body in position on the Cross, or, to use Tertullian's words, 'then is Peter girt by another when he is made fast to the cross' (*Scorp.* 15). The third phrase has to be taken in a different order when it applies to the hidden meaning, since the leading of Peter to the place of execution would come first.

The following verse (21.19) makes the reference to crucifixion quite definite, and it also co-ordinates the death of Peter with that of his Lord, 'Now this he spake, signifying by what manner of death he should glorify God.' This clearly points back to 12.33, 'But this he said, signifying by what manner of death he should die.'

Bishop Cassian in an article entitled 'John xxi' (*New Testament Studies* 3 [Jan. 1957], pp. 132–6) points out that 13.36 (that Peter would follow his Lord afterwards) looks forward to chapter 21, and that in three ways Peter is to follow: (*a*) as shepherd, (*b*) in his death, (*c*) in glorifying God by his death. If the argument of the present chapter is sound, we can perhaps add a fourth way in which Peter follows Jesus: (*d*) both of them in their death resemble Moses at Rephidim, for Peter stretched out his hands, and Jesus was in the midst of two others, 'on either side one'.

[1] Lagrange's note on this is particularly good.

THE MANNA AND THE BREAD OF LIFE

THE sixth chapter of John supplies one of the clearest examples of the importance of the wilderness imagery, and it need not detain us long. After the feeding of the five thousand we are in effect told that the people recognized in Jesus the second Moses. 'When therefore the people saw the sign which he did, they said: This is of a truth the prophet that cometh into the world' (6.14). As we saw in an earlier chapter, the following verse, describing the efforts of the people to make Jesus king, suggests that we have here the Messiah conceived along Mosaic lines, and not just 'the prophet' as a forerunner. It is relevant here to recall the Rabbinic evidence of the expectation that the Messiah, the second Deliverer, would repeat the signs of Moses, the first Deliverer.[1]

The matter is referred to again in verses 30 ff., particularly in the words, 'Our fathers ate the manna in the wilderness; as it is written, He gave them bread out of heaven to eat. Jesus therefore said unto them, Verily, verily, I say unto you, It was not Moses that gave you the bread out of heaven; but my Father giveth you the true bread out of heaven.' Here there is a double negation: (a) The gift of manna in the wilderness came not from Moses but from God; (b) the manna was not the true (alēthinos) bread from heaven which is now available in Jesus, who himself is the bread of life (6.35).

A passage from J. B. Lightfoot's *Biblical Essays* is worth quoting in this connexion:

The key to the meaning of the conversation is the fact that the Jews expected a miracle similar to the gift of manna in the wilderness, as an accompaniment of the appearance of the great deliverer. This expectation throws a flood of light on the whole discourse. But the

---

[1] Cf. the passage previously quoted from Koh. R. 1.9: 'What did the first redeemer? He brought down the manna. And the last Redeemer will bring down the manna.'

fact is not communicated in the passage itself. There is only a bald, isolated statement, which apparently is suggested by nothing, and itself fails to suggest anything: 'Our fathers did eat manna in the wilderness.' Then comes an aposiopesis. The inference is unexpressed. The expectation, which explains all, is left to be inferred, because it would be mentally supplied by men brought up among the ideas of the time. We ourselves have to get it by the aid of criticism and research from rabbinical authorities. But, when we have grasped it, we can unlock the meaning of the whole chapter.[1]

Hoskyns makes the point that Mark's account may possibly point in a similar direction: 'It may be that the Marcan account of the Feeding of the Five Thousand *in the desert* already contained the suggestion that the action of Jesus was the messianic counterpart of the miracle of Moses.'

Apart from the idea of a second Moses, the wider expectation of a second Exodus had led to the thought that the gifts of the wilderness period would be repeated in a heightened sense. This no doubt lies behind the 'hidden manna' of Rev. 2.17. A few other examples may be given. In 2 Baruch 29.8 it is said concerning the Messianic kingdom, 'And it shall come to pass at that self-same time that the treasury of manna shall again descend from on high, and they will eat of it in those years.' C. H. Dodd quotes (on p. 335) 'the fragment of a Sibylline Oracle cited in Theophilus *Ad Autolycum*, which may be pre-Christian': 'Those who fear God will inherit true and eternal life, themselves living for ever in the fertile garden of Paradise and feasting upon sweet bread from the starry heaven.' Again in the Mekhilta on Ex. 16.25 it is said of the manna, 'Ye shall not find it in this age, but ye shall find it in the age that is coming.'[2]

There is an interesting passage in the Midrash Rabbah on Ecclesiastes. In dealing with the words of Eccles. 11.1, 'Cast thy bread upon the waters', it refers to R. Eleazar b. R. Simai who 'interpreted the verse in connexion with the patriarch Abraham.

---

[1] P. 24. A similar passage from p. 152 is quoted by Bernard in his comments on John 6. On the previous page of Lightfoot's book (p. 151) he refers to the Moses/Messiah parallelism in Jewish teaching and says that 'the Rabbis carried out the parallelism into the most minute details, so that the career of the Messiah became in effect a reproduction of the career of Moses.' He is obviously drawing upon Gfrörer whom he mentions.

[2] Cf. also Tanchuma, Beshallach 21.66, quoted in Hoskyns. For other references see R. Meyer, Μάννα, *TWNT* IV, pp. 466 ff.

The Holy One, blessed be He, spake to him: You said, "and I will fetch a morsel of bread" (Gen. 18.5); I swear by your life that I will repay it to your descendants (*a*) in the wilderness, (*b*) in their settlement (in the holy land), and (*c*) in the Hereafter. In the wilderness, as it is said, Behold, I will cause it to rain bread from heaven for you (Ex. 16.4); in their settlement, as it is said, A land of wheat and barley (Deut. 8.8); in the Hereafter, as it is said, May he be as a rich cornfield in the land (Ps. 72.16).' The other three acts of kindness to his angelic visitors performed by Abraham (which do not concern us here) similarly bring, each one of them, a threefold reward: in the wilderness, in the settlement, and in the Hereafter.

In connexion with John 6 it must also be remembered that bread was a term used of the Jewish Torah, and behind this whole section is the implication that the law of Moses is now replaced by Jesus, who is himself the bread of life. The Rabbis applied the words of Prov. 9.5 ('Come, eat ye of my bread') to the Torah.[1] We have therefore in this chapter not only Jesus as the second Deliverer repeating the deeds of the first, but also the insistence which runs right through the book that the law of Moses has now been fulfilled and displaced by the Lord Jesus.

The Evangelist is concerned with something far more vital than the mere fulfilment of a Messianic sign or the feeding of the multitude. More important than any wonder in the regions near the sea of Galilee is the spiritual bread dwelt upon in the discourse in the synagogue. As C. H. Dodd points out, the early part of the discourse is roughly 'within the limits of Jewish eschatological beliefs which conceived the Messiah as a second Moses or . . . as a Moses-like figure sublimated or "etherialized"' (pp. 339 f.). But in the later parts of the discourse it is Christ himself who is the bread of life; and the further thought of mutual indwelling is developed and with this the Eucharistic associations of bread, matters which are beyond our immediate concern. The disciple lives because of Christ, as Christ lives because of the Father. This, of course, goes far beyond all Messianic expectations, Mosaic and otherwise.

[1] See the references in S.B. 2, pp. 483 f. on John 6.35.

VII

THE LIVING WATER AND THE ROCK

In this chapter we shall consider the words of Christ in John 7.37 f. at the Feast of Tabernacles, and one or two related references to water. After (1) discussing the interpretation of 7.37 and its connexion with the Feast and with the rock of the wilderness days, and (2) the punctuation of the two verses, upon which hinges whether we apply verse 38 to Christ or the believer, we shall refer (3) to the possible connexion with 19.34, the effusion from Christ's wounded side; then (4) a Jewish tradition concerning blood and water from the rock, and its bearing upon 19.34, will be considered; and (5) finally something must be said of the well of chapter 4 and of other water references in the Gospel.

1. In approaching John 7 we must remember that in the Old Testament and in later writings, the manna and the water from the rock are often linked together: e.g. Neh. 9.15, 'And gavest them bread from heaven[1] for their hunger, and broughtest forth water for them out of the rock for their thirst.' The bread and the waters are mentioned in the same verse (20) of Ps. 78; cf. the whole passage, verses 15-27, and also Ps. 105.40 f. Similarly in the New Testament, I Cor. 10.3 f., 'And did all eat the same spiritual food; and did all drink the same spiritual drink: for they drank of a spiritual rock that followed them: and the rock was Christ.'

As we have seen, John 6 presents Christ as the bread corresponding to the manna. It is therefore not surprising to find in chapter 7 the promise of living water, particularly in the context of the Feast of Tabernacles when the wilderness years were commemorated (see Lev. 23.42 f.). Though the smitten rock of Horeb is not mentioned in John 7.37 ff., the reference to this is widely recognized (Westcott, Lagrange, Loisy, Hoskyns and others).

[1] This is the phrase used in John 6. Neh. 9.15 is the passage cited in John 6.31.

The words of Hoskyns on 7.38 may be quoted. After referring to the Old Testament passages where the manna and the water out of the rock are associated he continues:

The author of the Gospel has already declared the fulfilment of the original gift of manna (6.31–5), and it is not unreasonable to suppose that he now proceeds to declare the fulfilment of the other great miracle of Moses. Jesus is the rock from which the true water flows forth for the salvation of the world (cf. I Cor. 10.4) as He is the Bread which came down from heaven and giveth life unto the world (6.33).

It is pretty generally agreed that the words of Christ in John 7.37–39 refer to the water ceremony carried out at the Feast of Tabernacles (Sukkoth). Water drawn from the pool of Siloam was poured at the altar into a silver bowl; this was carried out daily during the feast. (See in the Mishnah, Sukkah 4.9.) Another ceremony at this feast was the lighting of the candelabra, and this is probably the point of the reference in John 8.12, which will be considered in the next chapter. It was as though Jesus were claiming to be the fulfilment of what was foreshadowed in these two rites.

The water ceremony is thought to have originated in a quasi-magical attempt to ensure rain for the coming season, and prayers for rain are still associated with this feast.[1] Some authorities have maintained that the two ceremonies of water and light were in definite commemoration of the water from the smitten rock of Ex. 17 and Num. 20, and the light of the pillar of fire (Ex. 13). But there does not appear to be much Rabbinic evidence to this effect. According to other authorities the feast looked mainly forward rather than backwards; and there is no doubt that it was regarded eschatologically as anticipating the Messianic era. We know that a chapter sometimes read at Sukkoth was Zech. 14, which looks forward to the end of the days, when there would be abundance of water and light.[2] Further discussion may be found

---

[1] This connects with the New Year aspect and the renewal of creation; see H. Riesenfeld, *Jésus Transfiguré* (Copenhagen, 1947), pp. 25–27; H. Bornhäuser, *Sukka* (G. Beer and O. Holtzmann, *Die Mischna* II, 6, Giessen, 1935), pp. 136 f.

[2] Cf. H. Riesenfeld, *Jésus Transfiguré*, p. 37; R. G. Finch, *The Synagogue Lectionary and the New Testament* (1939), pp. 46 ff., where it is said that Zech. 14 was read every third year. In the Talmud, *Megillah* 31a: 'On the first day of Tabernacles we read the section of the festivals in Leviticus, and for haftarah,

in the additional note at the end of this chapter as to the Rabbinic evidence for a connexion between the water ceremony and the rock of the wilderness.

However, since the Feast of Tabernacles as a whole was a commemoration of the forty years in the wilderness, it would be natural to recall all the outstanding events of that period. In Lev. 23.42 f. it is said, 'Ye shall dwell in booths (*sukkoth*) seven days; all that are homeborn in Israel shall dwell in booths: that your generations may know that I made the children of Israel to dwell in booths, when I brought them out of the land of Egypt: I am the Lord your God.' It would therefore be difficult for those who witnessed the water ceremony to avoid thinking of the waters in the desert as well as the promised streams of the Messianic era especially as the latter were derived from the events of the desert period.

2. It is well known that there is a division of opinion about the punctuation of 7.37 f.; and some have favoured the view that the phrase 'he that believeth on me' should go with the preceding words:

> Let him that is athirst come unto me,
> And let him that believeth on me drink.

The saying would thus be similar in form to 6.35:

> He that cometh to me shall not hunger,
> And he that believeth on me shall never thirst.

One result of this punctuation is that verse 38 may be taken as a reference to Jesus and not to the believer: 'As the scripture hath said, From his belly shall flow rivers of living water.' This interpretation is favoured by Lagrange, Loisy, Dodd, Bultmann, Bauer, J. Jeremias and others.[1] It is interesting to note that while

---

Behold a day cometh for the Lord' (i.e. Zech. 14). Cf. also, I. Abrahams, *Studies in Pharisaism and the Gospels* II, p. 54; A. Guilding, *Fourth Gospel and Jewish Worship*, 1960, p. 94.

[1] Cf. the Jerusalem Bible (1956):
> Si quelqu'un a soif, qu'il vienne a moi
> et qu'il boive, celui qui croit en moi!

G. D. Kilpatrick also supports the connexion of the words 'he who believes in me' with the preceding words, *Journal of Theological Studies* II (1960), pp. 340–2.

Westcott in the first edition of his commentary referred verse 38 to the believer, following an interpretation which has been in favour since the time of Origen, there is a footnote in his later commentary on the Greek text (1908) where his son records, 'Bishop Westcott had intended to consider the interpretation of this passage more fully, and has indicated that he "now inclines" to interpret *autou* of Christ.'

It has been urged that verse 38 cannot refer to the believer because the next verse speaks of 'the Spirit, which they that believed on him were to *receive*', not 'to communicate'.[1]

Whichever punctuation be preferred, the reference of the whole passage 7.37 ff. to the water from the rock in the desert is not necessarily in doubt. But it should be observed that there is strong patristic support for seeing a reference to our Lord himself in verse 38. A letter from the Christians of Vienne and Lyons speaks of being refreshed and strengthened by the celestial fountain of living water that flows from the belly of Christ (Eusebius, *Hist. Eccl.* v.1) and though the word used is *nedus* and not *koilia* there is good ground for thinking that the passage was inspired by John 7.38. M. E. Boismard[2] has shown that Cyprian, Aphraates and Ephrem were among those who referred verse 38 to Christ, so that this is well represented in the Syriac and African churches. It is not an exclusively Western interpretation, as is sometimes alleged.

Quite apart from the punctuation, the whole passage may be compared with the words of Paul in I Cor. 10.4, 'they drank of the spiritual rock that followed them: and the rock was Christ.' It has been suggested that Paul's words may rest upon some such saying as is recorded in John 7.37 f. (cf. Cullmann, πέτρα, *TWNT* VI, p. 96).

3. Some of the commentators who refer verse 38 to Jesus think that this points forward to 19.34, when quite literally water came from the pierced side of Jesus (Loisy, Hoskyns, Dodd, p. 349). But as we have seen, the reference of 7.37 f. to the smitten rock does not depend upon the disputed punctuation and on more general grounds it has often been thought that the Evangelist

[1] So E. G. King in *The Yalkut on Zechariah*, 1882, p. 120.
[2] 'De son ventre couleront des fleuves d'eau', *Revue Biblique* 65 (Oct. 1958), pp. 523–46.

wishes us to see in the water from the wounded side of Christ the fulfilment of the water from the smitten rock of the wilderness. This is the implication of the well-known words of Toplady's verse:

> Rock of Ages, cleft for me
> Let me hide myself in Thee.
> Let the water and the blood
> From Thy riven side which flowed,
> Be of sin the double cure,
> Save me from its guilt and power.

Thirty years before Toplady's hymn, Charles Wesley wrote several with a similar thought; and indeed one began with the words, 'Rock of Israel, cleft for me'. Another beginning 'O Rock of our salvation' went on to speak of the mingled stream of blood and water. This was no doubt inspired by some words from Brevint's *The Christian Sacrament and Sacrifice*:

O Rock of Israel, Rock of Salvation, Rock struck and cleft for me, let those two streams of blood and water which once gushed out of Thy side bring down pardon and holiness into my soul; and let me thirst after them now, as if I stood upon the mountain whence sprung this water, and near the cleft of that rock, the wounds of my Lord, whence gushed this sacred blood.

There is a long tradition linking John 19.34 with the rock of the desert. Matthew Henry's commentary in its note on this verse includes the words, 'Now was the rock smitten (I Cor. 10.4), now was the fountain opened (Zech. 13.1) . . .'[1]

A few examples may be given to show that some of the Fathers saw this same connexion:

(a) Cyprian (*Epistle* 63.8) quotes Isa. 48.21 which speaks of waters flowing out of the rock and says that this was fulfilled in the Gospel, when Christ who is the rock was 'opened'[2] by the

---

[1] Similarly E. C. Selwyn wrote in reference to John 19.34, 'Christ, the Rock of Ages, is smitten and pierced': *Journal of Theological Studies* 13 (O.S.) (1911–12), p. 240.

[2] Cyprian reads in 19.34 'opened' instead of 'pierced'. This is the reading of both the Old Latin and the Vulgate (followed by Wyclif and the Rheims version). It may be due to the Greek being read as ἤνοιξεν. There may also be some connexion with Zech. 13.1 ('In that day there shall be a fountain opened to the house of David'), Zech. 12.10 being quoted a little later in John 19 (verse 37).

thrust of the spear in his Passion. Christ himself, he continues, recalls the prophet's prediction in his words of 7.37 f.

(*b*) An anonymous treatise on re-baptism, probably belonging to the third century (sometimes associated with Cyprian's period: see Ante-Nicene Christian Library, vol. 13, Edinburgh, 1869, pp. 401 ff.) may be referred to here, since it makes quite explicit the connexion between John 7.38 and 19.34 in the words: 'Every one who thirsts may come and drink, as says the Scripture, "From his belly flowed rivers of living water"; which rivers were manifested first of all in the Lord's passion, when from his side, pierced by the soldier's spear, flowed blood and water . . .' (Although the rock is not mentioned in this passage it is relevant as supporting the connexion between 7.38 and 19.34.)

(*c*) In the article referred to above by M. E. Boismard it is shown that Aphraates and Ephrem associate together 7.38 and 19.34 and see in the latter the fulfilment of the rock struck by Moses.

(*d*) Origen, in his *Homilies on Exodus*, when dealing with the rock in the wilderness (XI.2) points out that it yielded water only when struck; and so Christ, he goes on, caused the streams of the New Covenant to flow when he was struck and hung on the Cross. It was necessary that he should be smitten, for if this had not taken place and the water and blood had not issued from his side, we should all suffer a thirst for the word of God.

(*e*) Gregory of Nyssa similarly in his *Life of Moses* II refers to the rock smitten by Moses and finds the fulfilment in John 19.34 (section 270; see *Sources chrétiennes*, edited by H. de Lubac and J. Daniélou, No. 1). In a footnote on this passage Daniélou urges (rightly, I think) that this thought was in the mind of the Evangelist.

In an illuminating passage, E. A. Abbott has called attention to the two occasions in John when Jesus spoke of his thirst. He places side by side the words to the Samaritan woman, 'Give me to drink' (4.7) and the words from the Cross, 'I thirst'; and after quoting 19.34–37 he writes:

The Son, in bearing thirst, bears it for others, calling forth faith from the woman of Samaria, and kindness from the soldiers round the Cross. In the former case there follows the gift of the living water to

Samaria; in the latter, the vision of the mingled blood and water that are to satisfy the thirst of all mankind.[1]

This shows true insight into the Evangelist's symbolism.

4. We turn now to a remarkable Jewish tradition concerning the rock which also has a bearing upon the piercing of our Lord's side. Westcott drew attention to it, deriving his information from John Lightfoot's *Horae Hebraicae* (seventeenth century): 'Lightfoot quotes a remarkable tradition from "Shemoth R." 122a, based on the interpretation of Ps. 78.20 . . . that "Moses struck the rock twice, and first it gushed out blood and then water".' Shemoth R. is, of course, the part of the Midrash Rabbah devoted to Exodus, and is nowadays usually referred to as Exodus R. More recent commentators have paid little attention to this; Billerbeck quotes the Lightfoot passage, but does not consider it to be relevant. But if on other grounds we have reached the conclusion that 19.34 is to be connected with the smitten rock, it is surely not a mere coincidence that water and blood are associated both with the rock and with Christ crucified.

Exodus R. quotes Ps. 78.20 ('He smote the rock and the waters gushed out') and points out that the word for 'gushed out' 'signifies nothing else but blood', since it is used with this meaning in Lev. 15.20; it concludes that the twofold smiting of the rock produced first blood and then water. After quoting these words Lightfoot continues: 'The rock was Christ (I Cor. 10.4). Compare these two together: Moses smote the rock; and blood and water, saith the Jew, flowed out thence:—The soldiers pierced our Saviour's side with a spear; and water and blood, saith the Evangelist, flowed thence.' He affirms that the words of John 19.35 ('that ye also may believe') mean, 'that you may believe that this is the true blood of the new covenant, which so directly answers the type in the confirmation of the old'.

This is not the only Rabbinic reference to this effect. The Palestinian Targum says, 'and Moses lifted up his hand, and with his rod struck the rock twice: at the first time it dropped blood; but at the second time there came forth a multitude of waters' (Targum on Num. 20.11).

Once we see that the rock imagery lies behind John 7.37 ff. and

---

[1] *Diatessarica* 10.iii, 1915, p. 206.

19.34, and that water from the rock-Christ is spoken of in I Cor. 10.4, it is surely clear that the Rabbinic water and blood tradition is relevant. No comment on 19.34 is complete without reference to this tradition, as Boismard points out in *Revue Biblique* 63 (1956), pp. 271 f.[1]

If the rock imagery lies behind 19.34, it will be seen that any theological interpretation should bring out 'drinking' rather than 'being baptized'. St Paul in I Cor. 10.1–4 connects baptism with the cloud and the sea, and drinking with the 'spiritual rock'. So also in John 7.37 ff.

5. The influence of the wilderness experiences can be traced in other Johannine references to water. In connexion with John 4 we must recall the song of the well in Num. 21.17 f. (verse 16 shows that it is the water from the smitten rock which is being celebrated).

> Then sang Israel this song:
> Spring up, O well; sing ye unto it:
> The well, which the princes digged,
> Which the nobles of the people delved,
> With the sceptre, and with their staves.

Bentzen suggests that this may be classed with Workers' Songs, and the allusion is to a well hallowed by legends like those of Ex. 17.6; Num. 20.11. 'But it has been reinterpreted by the redactor who brought it into the present context.'[2] Lods thinks that the poem is a prayer addressed to a holy well, and a hymn in praise of it. We are not concerned, however, at the moment with the question of its origin, but its final place in the story and the use made of it in Jewish thought.

It is unusual for a well to spring up; it is as though the well were confused with a fountain. But the tradition probably lies behind the words of John 4.14, 'a well of water springing up

---

[1] W. A. Heidel in an article on Vergil's Messianic expectations in the *American Journal of Philology* (45 [1924], pp. 205–37) refers to the Targum on the blood and water and continues, 'Christians, from Paul onward, saw in the rock of Meribah a type of Christ, whose blood is drunk in the wine of the eucharist: hence it was doubtless regarded as especially significant that when His side was struck and pierced at the Crucifixion by the soldier's spear, "straightway there came out blood and water".'

[2] *Introduction to the Old Testament* (Copenhagen, 1952), Part I, p. 125; see also Appendix 7.

unto eternal life'. The Greek word ἅλλομαι is nowhere, I think, used of a well except in this passage and in references inspired by it. The idea has passed into Christian hymnology as in the lines, 'Spring Thou up within my heart, Rise to all eternity' from Charles Wesley's 'Jesu, Lover of my soul'. Sometimes the language of Num. 21 reappears as we can see in the line from another hymn, 'Spring up, O well, in heavenly power.'

The song of the well was frequently quoted in Rabbinic writings. In the Midrash Rabbah alone there are thirteen references to it in the index. It appears in the Zadokite Fragment, 8.4 ff., with an interesting interpretation: 'The *well* is the Law, and those who dug it are the captivity of Israel, who went out from the land of Judah and sojourned in the land of Damascus, all of whom God called *princes*, because they sought him, and their glory was not rejected in the mouth of anyone. And the *staff* (or legislator) is he who studies the law, as Isaiah said, "He produces an instrument for his work." And the *nobles* of the people are those who come to dig the well with the staves (or rules) which the staff (or legislator) prescribed to walk in during the whole period of wickedness; and without them they shall not attain to the arising of him who will teach righteousness at the end of days.'

It is important to notice that 'the well is the law', an interpretation in line with Rabbinic symbolism.[1] In John 4 it is Jesus who offers men a well of water springing up; this is another example of Christ and his gifts replacing the law. As C. H. Dodd points out, 'In Talmud and Midrash the Torah is constantly compared to water' (p. 83); he is speaking, in the context, of the contrast between the Torah and the incarnate Word, as one of the governing ideas of the Fourth Gospel.

Another allusion in John 4 may take us back to the Horeb story of Ex. 17.1–7. The narrative speaks of Jacob's well (4.6), which is nowhere mentioned in the Old Testament; it also says that Jacob 'drank thereof himself, and his sons, and his cattle' (4.12). Here again this fact is not mentioned in the Old Testament concerning Jacob personally. But in Ex. 17.3 the people (Israel) say, 'Wherefore hast thou brought me up out of Egypt, to kill *me and my sons and my cattle with thirst?*' This is the literal translation of the Hebrew, the plural of the versions ('us') being due to

[1] Cf. S.B. 2, pp. 435 f., on John 4.10.

the translators. When we see that this comes from the story of the water from the smitten rock (Ex. 17.1–7) we may suspect that the wording of John 4.12 is not just a coincidence.

A further interesting point about John 4 is that there are a few reminiscences of Gen. 24, the story of Isaac's servant and Rebekah by the well:

Gen. 24.16 and she went down to the fountain, and filled her pitcher.

    17 the servant . . . said, Give me to drink (cf. John 4.7).

    26 and 48 refer to worship (cf. John 4.20 ff.).

    28–32 the damsel ran, and told her mother's house according to these words (cf. John 4.28, the woman left her water-pot and went into the city).

    Laban constrains the visitor to remain with them (cf. John 4.40).

    33 And there was set meat before him to eat: but he said, I will not eat, until I have told mine errand (cf. John 4.31–34, where Jesus prefers instead of meat the doing of his Father's will, 'the will of him that sent me').

The following words from the LXX of Gen. 24 recur in John 4: γυνή—πηγή—ἐκπορεύομαι—ἀντλῆσαι[1]—ὕδωρ—ὑδρία—μένειν. Incidentally the Midrash Rabbah on Gen. 24 associates Num. 21.17 with the words of verse 16, 'she went down to the fountain, and filled her pitcher'. It declares that 'the water ascended as soon as it saw her'.

Mention may be made at this point of the prominence of water in the Fourth Gospel, especially in the early chapters. The following instances do not exhaust the list: baptizing with water and the Spirit (1.25–33); changing water to wine (2.1 ff.); born of water and the Spirit (3.5); John baptizing 'because there was much water there' (3.22 ff.); the well of Sychar and the water of life (4); the man at the pool (5.2 ff.); rivers of living water (7.37 ff.); the blind man sent to wash in the pool of Siloam (9.7, 11, 15); the feet-washing (13); the blood and water (19.34). Some of these are

[1] In connexion with this word it may be recalled that John has many links with Tabernacles, which included as one of its most prominent rites 'the Water-drawing' (Sukkah 4.9 to 5.1; Danby, p. 179). Drawing water occurs in John 2.8 f., 'the servants which had drawn the water', and 4.7, 11 and 15.

related to John's baptism; and possibly some, by indirect ways, to Qumran lustrations; others to the purifications of the Jews, as definitely stated in 2.6. In all these cases there is a contrast between Judaism and what Christ has brought.

Additional Note

A number of commentators and expositors, both old and new, maintain that the water ceremony at the Feast of Tabernacles was in definite commemoration of the water from the smitten rock of Ex. 17 and Num. 20. It is of interest that the great John Lightfoot in his *Horae Hebraicae* does not make this point, as he had evidently found no Rabbinic evidence to this effect, nor does Matthew Henry, who had studied Lightfoot to great advantage. Last century a number of commentators, e.g. Bishop Wordsworth, maintained that this was the meaning of the water ceremony. His contemporary, Dean Alford, was more cautious and in his comment on John 7.37 conceded that the water ceremony 'was by some supposed—as the dwelling in tabernacles represented their life in the desert of old—to refer to the striking of the rock by Moses'; but he went on to give other explanations of the passage. Westcott has the following:

> The pouring out of the water (like the use of the great lights, 8.12) was a commemoration of one conspicuous detail of the life in the wilderness typified by the festival.

Godet's note is similar.

Is there any Rabbinic evidence that the water ceremony was regarded in this way? One Jewish authority whom I approached on this point told me he knew of none, and I have never seen any conclusive and specific reference quoted. However, I have subsequently noticed that in the Tosephta this connexion appears to be made. We read in Tos. Sukkah 3.3, 'Whence is the name "Water Gate"? It is so called because through it they take the flask of water used for the libation at the Feast. R. Eliezer ben Jacob says of it, "The waters are dripping" (Ezek. 47.2), intimating that *water oozing out and rising, as if from this flask*, will in future days come forth from under the threshold of the Temple.'[1] Much more is then said of the waters described in Ezek. 47 as

[1] As translated by A. W. Greenup (*Sukkah, Mishna and Tosefta,* in SPCK Translations of Early Documents, Series 3, 1925); my italics.

destined to flow from beneath the Temple threshold, and this is still the theme in 3.10 which concludes with the quotation of Ezek. 47.8–12 and the words, 'intimating that all "the waters of creation" will come forth as from the mouth of this flask.'

The paragraph which immediately follows begins:

3.11. So the well, which was with Israel in the wilderness, was like a rock of the size of a k'bara (i.e. a large round vessel), and was *oozing out and rising as from the mouth of this flask*, travelling with them up the mountains and going down with them to the valleys. Wherever Israel encamped it encamped opposite them before the door of the Tabernacle. The princes of Israel with their staves[1] surrounded it and said over it this song, Spring up, o well, sing ye unto it (Num. 21.17). Then the waters bubbled forth, and rose on high like a pillar; and every one drew out the staff of his tribe and family, as it is said,

> The well which the princes digged,
> Which the nobles of the people delved,
> With the sceptre and with their staves (Num. 21.18).

Paragraphs 3.12 and 13 are also on the subject of the wilderness waters. It can surely be claimed that here the flask used at the feast of Sukkah is definitely associated with the wilderness waters. The same phrase, italicized above, occurs both in 3.3 and 3.11, in one place speaking of the flask used at the feast and in the other of the wilderness experience. This confirms that in the minds of some Jews at least the two were associated. Incidentally this context gives a particularly clear example of the tradition (known to St Paul, I Cor. 10.4) that the rock accompanied the people.[2]

[1] Greening's translation gives 'slaves', but his Hebrew text (Texts for Students 31, 1921) makes it clear that this is an error for 'staves'.

[2] Cf. the Jerusalem Targum (pseudo-Jonathan) on Num. 21.17–20; see also J. W. Doeve, *Jewish Hermeneutics in the Synoptic Gospels and Acts*, pp. 110 f.

VIII

THE LIGHT OF THE WORLD AND THE THREE GIFTS

THE insertion of the passage concerning the woman taken in adultery (John 7.53–8.11, which, as the oldest manuscripts show, is an intrusion here), as well as the chapter division, has obscured the fact that 8.12 ff. is a continuation of the Tabernacles episode. As a number of commentators have seen, the saying about light is to be connected with the candlestick ceremony which took place at Tabernacles, just as the words about water (7.37 ff.) are linked with the water ceremony. Mention of the treasury (8.20) is another link with the light ritual, since the treasury was adjacent to the women's court, where this ceremony took place.

The nightly celebration is thus described by Joseph Hochman in his *Jerusalem Temple Festivities:*[1]

The Women's Hall was illuminated with golden candlesticks reaching over the height of the walls, and crowned by four golden lamps, each of which was reached by a ladder; at the bottom of every ladder stood a son of the priests who held permanent office in the Temple, with a pitcher of 30 (?) 'logs' of oil, from which he fed the lamp in his charge. The wicks for the lamps were provided from the worn-out breeches and girdles of the common priests, which were torn up into strips and plaited into wicks for the illumination of the festival, and placed in the bowls that served as lamps, over the brims of which their burning ends hung down, no doubt from spouts provided for the purpose.

According to the Mishnah, on which this account is mainly based, 'there was not a courtyard in Jerusalem that did not reflect the light . . .' (Sukkah 5.3). 'Men of piety and good works used to dance before them with burning torches in their hands, singing songs and praises' (5.4).

Zech. 14 was, as we have seen, one of the passages of the

[1] 1908, p. 75.

lectionary for Tabernacles, and this has an eschatological reference to light as well as water.

Some commentators have affirmed that the light ceremony at
Tabernacles was in commemoration of the pillar of fire in the
wilderness. I know of no Rabbinic evidence to this effect; and
a learned Rabbi whom I have consulted on this point is unac-
quainted with any reference of this kind. However, the statement
is still made occasionally. Last century F. Godet (of whose work
on the Fourth Gospel Westcott thought very highly) wrote on
8.12, 'he looks beyond the candelabra to the miraculous act of
which it was the memorial':

That which really concerns us is the meaning of the feast of Tabernacles, which the people had met to keep. This feast was designed to
commemorate the favours they had received from God during their
sojourn in the wilderness. Hence the booths of foliage. Now among
these favours, the two chief were the water from the rock and the
pillar of fire. Jesus had just applied to Himself one of these types. He
now appropriates the other (hence the πάλιν, v. 12).

He that followeth me . . . refers not, as some have thought, to the
torch dance which took place in the court, but to the wandering of
Israel in the wilderness. They arose, advanced, stopped, encamped at
the signal of the fiery cloud. With such a guide, the travellers knew no
darkness.[1]

Similarly Westcott affirms that the lamps at the feast were 'only
images of the pillar of light, which had guided the people in the
wilderness. . . . And it is to this finally that the words of the
Lord refer. The idea of that light of the Exodus—transitory and
partial—was now fulfilled in the living Light of the world.'

In spite of the lack of Rabbinic evidence to support this, it
could be urged that as the feast as a whole recalled the wilderness
years, the light would inevitably bring to remembrance the
guiding pillar of flame. There is force in this, and even if the light

---

[1] This is an appropriate point at which to mention another passage in
which Godet gathers up a number of wilderness references in this Gospel:
'He (Christ) had represented Himself . . . in ch. 3 as the true brazen serpent,
in 6 as the bread of heaven; in 7 He is the true rock; in 8 the true life-giving
cloud, and so on till 19 when He will at length realize the type of the Paschal
Lamb' (Eng. trans., 1886, p. 294).

ceremony had quite a different origin, it might all the same arouse associations of this kind.[1]

However, we may leave these surmises on one side, because there is a much better way of approaching the interpretation of John 8.12 by considering the *three gifts* so frequently referred to in Jewish writings.

In the Old Testament itself, the manna, the water and the pillar of fire are at times linked together. Neh. 9.12 reads, 'Moreover thou leddest them in a pillar of cloud by day; and in a pillar of fire by night, to give them light in the way wherein they should go', while verse 15 refers to the 'bread from heaven' and the water from the rock. Similarly in Ps. 105, verse 39 mentions the cloud and the fire, verse 40 deals with the bread of heaven, and verse 41 the waters from the rock.

In later traditions the three gifts were associated with Moses, Aaron and Miriam respectively. The Mekhilta on Ex. 16.28–36 says that when Miriam died the well was taken away; when Aaron died the cloud of glory was taken away; when Moses died the manna ceased. The full account of R. Joshua quoted here says that when Miriam died the well was taken away, but it then came back because of the merits of Moses and Aaron; when Aaron died the cloud of glory was taken away, but it came back because of the merits of Moses; when Moses died, all three, the well, the cloud of glory and the manna, were taken away and returned no more. One or two other references may be given. Numbers R. 1.2 says that the manna was due to the merit of Moses, the clouds of glory were due to the merit of Aaron, and the well was due to the merit of Miriam. Here again we find that the manna ceased when Moses died (Josh. 5.12), the clouds of glory when Aaron died (Num. 21.4), and the waters ceased when Miriam died (Num. 20.1 f.). Similarly in Song R. 4.5 the statement is attributed to R. Jose that 'three good patrons arose for Israel, viz. Moses, Aaron and Miriam, and for the sake of them three precious gifts

---

[1] H. Bornhäuser favours the theory that the light ceremony is to be connected with the renewing of the sun's light at the beginning of the year; Tabernacles was, of course, a new year feast (Beer and Holtzmann's *Die Mischna* II.6 *Sukka,* pp. 154 f.). J. G. Frazer's *Golden Bough* gives illustrations of New Year torch ceremonies to ensure the renewal of the sun's light. Cf. H. Riesenfeld's *Jésus Transfiguré,* pp. 26 f., 113; he is, however, thinking mainly of the nightly torch ceremonies at the feast.

were bestowed on Israel, the well, the manna, the clouds of glory.'
(Cf. also Lev. R. 27.6.)

It will thus be seen that whatever may have been the meaning
of the Tabernacles light ceremony, we have grounds for linking
John 8.12 with the pillar of fire from a consideration of the 'three
gifts'. We have already seen that John finds in Christ the counterpart of the manna (ch. 6) and the water from the rock (ch. 7 and
elsewhere). In 8.12 occur the words which are occupying us in
the present section: 'Again therefore Jesus spake unto them, saying, I am the light of the world: he that followeth me shall not
walk in the darkness, but shall have the light of life.' These words
are sometimes interpreted in terms of the sun; but no one
'follows' the sun when he walks; and while we cannot press this
point as decisive it nevertheless brings greater consistency into
the whole context when we think of the fiery pillar of the wilderness giving its guiding light to those who followed.[1] If this is
the correct interpretation it will be seen that in John 6, 7 and 8
we have the Christian fulfilments of the three great wilderness
gifts.

There are a few patristic references which show that the pillar
of fire was regarded as a type of Christ; and even though John
8.12 is not quoted, these passages give support to the interpretation of the Johannine passage which we are here advocating.
Ambrose in his work on the Sacraments says that the column of
light corresponds to Christ, the column of cloud to the Holy
Spirit (Migne, *PL* 16, 420 ff.). Zeno of Verona[2] has a series of
sermonettes on Exodus in which he expounds the spiritual meaning as applied to the Church; and in one of these he writes, 'colum-
na viam demonstrans Christus est Dominus' (*PL* 11, 509 f.).

Light is, of course, one of the major themes of this Gospel,
right from the opening verses (1.4 ff.). And, just as in the case
of the bread and the water, we have here another symbol identified
in Jewish teaching with the Torah; and again the Gospel affirms
that the true light is Christ. In all these three important connexions, Christ is set over against the Torah. This is one of the

---

[1] Cf. Lampe and Woollcombe, *Essays on Typology* (SBT 22), 1957, p. 47;
the Jerusalem Bible, footnote on John 8.12; J. Daniélou, *Sacramentum
Futuri*, p. 139.
[2] Cf. J. Daniélou, *op. cit.*, p. 156.

main themes of the Prologue; and in this particular context it is interesting to recall that in the Assumption of Moses the Torah is described as the light that lighteth every man.[1]

Another consideration is that the pillar of cloud and fire was expected to return in the end-time; cf. Isa. 4.5 f.; 1 Baruch 5.8 f.; Song R. on 1.8 (R. Akiba). John insists that this and other eschatological gifts are now available in Christ. It may possibly be significant that the darkness at Calvary is not mentioned in John.

The imagery of the three gifts is clearly maintained in Christian thought, though they are not always found in close association with one another. But one striking example shows how, quite unconsciously, the wilderness trinity comes to carry a Christian meaning. The well-known pilgrim hymn, 'Guide me, O Thou great Jehovah' (W. Williams), contains in adjacent lines references to the manna, the water and the fiery pillar:

> Bread of heaven!
> Feed me now and evermore.
>
> Open Thou the crystal fountain,
> Whence the healing stream shall flow;
> Let the fiery, cloudy pillar ,
> Lead me all my journey through.

[1] Cf. an article by the present writer, 'John 1.9 and a Rabbinic tradition', *Zeitschrift für neutestamentliche Wissenschaft* 49 (1958), pp. 288 ff. On the Torah as light see S.B.2, p. 357 on John 1.4.

IX

'WE BEHELD HIS GLORY' (John 1.14)

In this chapter we shall first look at the words of 1.14, with special references to possible reminiscences of the wilderness days, the Tabernacle and the glory. We shall then recall the Synoptic story of the Transfiguration and suggest that in the Fourth Gospel the whole ministry of Christ, and not just an isolated occasion, is presented as the manifestation of his glory; and this discussion will bring to light once again a contrast between Jesus and Moses.

It has often been urged that the word used in 1.14 (the verb *skēnoō*) is a veiled reference to the Tabernacle (*skēnē*); in fact, the RVm gives the translation 'tabernacled among us'. The words of Ex. 25.8 may be recalled, 'and let them make me a sanctuary; that I may *dwell among them*'. John 1.14 says the Word 'dwelt among us'. The Hebrew verb used in Ex. 25 is *shaken*. Both Delitzsch and the version of Ginsberg and Salkinson use the Hebrew word *shaken* in translating John 1.14. The divine presence which was associated with the Tabernacle came in later times to be known as the Shekinah, which, of course, comes from the same root. It may be that the Evangelist uses the word *skēnoō* because it has the same consonants as *shaken* and *Shekinah*; but in any case it is related to *skēnē* (tabernacle).[1]

There is also here undoubtedly a reference to the Wisdom literature, especially to Ecclus. 24.8, where Wisdom is the speaker: 'So the Creator of all things gave me a commandment, and he that made me caused my tabernacle to rest, and said, Tabernacle (*kataskēnoō*) in Jacob and let thine inheritance be in Israel.' Verse 10 in the same chapter speaks of Wisdom ministering in the holy Tabernacle. As Rendel Harris has shown,[2] a good deal of the phraseology of the Prologue can be paralleled from what is said

---

[1] *Skēnoō* is, of course, a perfectly good Greek word used by classical writers; the word by itself does not compel any association with the Old Testament tabernacle.

[2] *The Origin of the Prologue to St John's Gospel*, Cambridge, 1917.

65

by Jewish writers concerning the Wisdom of God (particularly in Prov. 8; Wisdom of Solomon, and Ecclesiasticus); but it must be remembered that the Jews had identified Wisdom with Torah, and it is likely that the Prologue's main interest is to show how Christ takes the place of the Torah; all that had been claimed for the latter is here ascribed to the Logos-Son of God.[1] The passage we have just quoted from Ecclus. 24 comes from a sustained hymn in praise of Wisdom, in which she is clearly identified with the Torah; cf. verses 23 f.: 'The *law* which Moses commanded as a heritage for the assemblies of Jacob, which filleth men with *wisdom* like Pison. . . .' Nevertheless this does not involve the abandonment of the wilderness reference; indeed, as we have just seen, Wisdom was herself (in Ecclus. 24) brought into connexion with 'the holy Tabernacle'.

Lagrange has an excellent note on 1.14 in which he points out that the words 'among us' recall how God was present in the midst of Israel in the wilderness period and after. He claims that this helps to explain John's choice of a word about living in a tent. The divine presence, he continues, was made manifest by the cloud, which was associated both with the Tabernacle (Ex. 33.7–11) and later with the Temple (I Kings 8.10 f.). Thus arose the doctrine of the 'Shekinah', a term which the Targums used at times as a synonym for God himself; cf. Lev. 26.12, where the Targum reads, 'I will cause my Shekinah to dwell among you.'

The dwelling in tents or booths (*sukkoth*) was a prominent feature of the wilderness days; and once a year at the most joyous of Jewish feasts the people were ordered to dwell in booths for seven days in commemoration of this historic period (Lev. 23.42). Moreover, during the forty years' wandering the Lord himself was in the midst of his people, dwelling like them in a tent or Tabernacle. If St John's Gospel is specially interested in the wilderness days it might be expected that some reference would be made to the Feast of Tabernacles, and to the divine Tabernacle of testimony. Both these expectations are fulfilled. The Feast of Tabernacles holds a prominent place in the narrative (chs. 7–8), and as we have already seen in earlier chapters, various items of its

---

[1] Cf. λέγω, *TWNT* IV, pp. 138 ff., a discussion of Logos and Torah in the Prologue. This matter will be taken up and amplified in chapter XIII, 'Christ and the Torah'.

ritual are given a Christian meaning. And as for the Tabernacle itself, this appears to be hinted at in 1.14, the passage we are now considering.

Mention has been made of the fact that the Feast of Tabernacles had an eschatological reference, as well as an historical one; and this must be borne in mind in interpreting John 1.14. The Tabernacle in the midst of the tents of Israel was an open manifestation that the Lord was in the midst of his people. Ezekiel and others looked forward to the time when again it would be said, 'The Lord is there' (Ezek. 48.35). In St John this is a present reality in the Word made flesh.

Christian thought has sometimes seen a link between the Feast of Tabernacles and the Incarnation, and there is warrant for this in John 1.14. Christopher Wordsworth in his commentary of a hundred years ago wrote on this verse: 'The Tabernacle of our Humanity became the Shekinah of Deity. . . . As the Feast of the Passover was a type of Christ's Passion, and the Feast of Pentecost was a figure of the sending of the Holy Ghost, so the Feast of Tabernacles seems to have been typical of Christ's Incarnation.'[1]

It will be recalled that *the glory of God* was often associated with the nomadic sanctuary; and as it was with the original Tabernacle, so it was with the fulfilment: 'he tabernacled among us and we beheld his glory.' In this connexion it should be remembered that among the wilderness features expected to return in Messianic times was the cloud of glory; cf. Isa. 4.5 f.:

And the Lord will create over the whole habitation of mount Zion, and over her assemblies, a cloud and smoke by day, and the shining of a flaming fire by night. . . .

Again in II Macc. 2 there is a description of Jeremiah hiding the Tabernacle in a cave on mount Horeb with the ark and the altar of incense, and declaring that the place

shall be unknown until the time that God gather his people again together, and receive them unto mercy. Then shall the Lord shew

---

[1] In a somewhat similar way Westcott in his commentary on Hebrews (1889) in an additional note on the general significance of the Tabernacle (pp. 233–40) maintains that the humanity of Christ is the archetypal Tabernacle; he reaches this conclusion without any reference to John 1.14.

them these things, and the glory of the Lord shall appear, and the cloud also, as it was shewed under Moses, and as when Solomon desired that the place might be honourably sanctified (7–8).

The implication of John 1.14 is that again the Tabernacle of God is with men and the eschatological glory is present in Christ.

A brief but striking quotation from F. B. Meyer will serve to gather up what has been said about the Incarnation and the glory, and to point forward to a consideration of the Transfiguration:

The Tabernacle was a material representation of the great truth of the Incarnation. It was made after the pattern of the nature of our Lord. which, as the sublime antitype, was eternally present to the mind and thought of God. Well then might Jesus speak in the same breath of the temple and of his body (2.21) . . .

We are the pilgrim host. Our bodies are but frail, shifting tabernacles, to be as easily dissolved as a tent is struck (II Cor. 5.1),[1] and amidst us has been reared the true Tabernacle, which God has pitched and not man. . . .

There were times when the light that shone in the most holy place could not be confined there; but issued forth, and flooded the entire structure so that the multitudes without could discern its splendour. And so in the earthly life of our blessed Lord there were moments when the glory of the Only-begotten of the Father broke through the limitations which He had assumed, and bathed his mortal body in transcendent light and beauty. Such a season was the Transfiguration, when even his garments became white as the light.[2]

It is at first sight surprising that John should omit all reference to the incident of the Transfiguration. It may be that to him the manifestation of Christ's glory was not an isolated event, for he says concerning the whole ministry, 'We saw his glory.'[3] Like the Transfiguration glory (Mark 9.9) it was seen by the disciples and not by the world. A brief reference to the significance of the Synoptic story will not be out of place here. Much has been written about this and the various theories are not necessarily exclusive of one another.

[1] Meyer's reference to II Cor. 5.1 would be all the more appropriate if that epistle was written (as T. W. Manson held) near the time of the Feast of Tabernacles. W. D. Davies accepts the suggestion, *Paul and Rabbinic Judaism*, 1948, p. 313.

[2] *Life and Light of Men*, pp. 29 f.

[3] Cf. Barrett, p. 44; Dodd, p. 207 note 2; A. M. Ramsey, *The Glory of God and the Transfiguration of Christ*, 1949, pp. 123 f.

It is probable that Moses and Elijah were expected as the Messiah's forerunners; and the incident shows how these two fulfilled this expectation. The two witnesses of Rev. 11, who show characteristics respectively of Moses and Elijah, provide evidence of the existence of this tradition in the first century. There is also the well-known passage in Deut. R. 3.17: 'In the world to come when I bring unto them Elijah the prophet, the two of you (Moses and Elijah) shall come together.'[1]

But another motif of the Transfiguration story is concerned with the glory of Moses and the glory of Christ. The incident of the shining of Moses' face (Ex. 34.29 ff.) had made a great impression on the Jews; it bore witness to the closeness of his communion with God. Thus the Targum of Onkelos says in this place, 'Moses knew not how great was the splendour of the glory of his countenance'; and the Jerusalem Targum, 'Moses knew not that the visage (form) of his face shone with the splendour which had come upon him from the brightness of the glory of the Lord's Shekinah in the time of his speaking with him.' The early Christians in their disputes with the Jews would be concerned to show that the glory of Christ was greater than the glory of Moses. Several passages in the New Testament deal with the subject of 'Moses and Jesus and glory'—Heb. 3.1–6 ('worthy of more glory than Moses'), II Cor. 3.1–18 and 4.1–6, which deals specifically with Ex. 34 and the greater glory of the new dispensation, and the transfiguration incident itself (Mark 9.2–8 and parallels).[2] Some years ago, when considering these three passages and their common theme, the present writer surmised that in early debates the Jews may have pointed out that the shining of Moses' face was a divine vindication of his close connexion with God; had anything of this kind happened to Jesus? Later he found a Jewish saying making this very point. A medieval work named *Nizzachon* refers to 'Moses of blessed memory', who spoke face to face with God and whose countenance was so luminous that the people were afraid to approach him; it goes on to say concerning Jesus that 'he was not endowed with any splendour,

---

[1] Cf. above, p. 27, and the reference there to Boobyer.
[2] Heb. 3.5–6 emphasizes that Jesus was a son, Moses a servant; cf. Mark 9.7, 'This is my beloved Son; hear ye him.'

but was just like the rest of men. Wherefore it is manifest that one ought not to believe in him.'[1]

The glory of Moses is not dealt with directly in John; but as indicated earlier (in ch. 2) there is a contrast between Moses and Christ in the Prologue (1.17) in the section which emphasizes the glory of the latter. The words 'No man hath seen God at any time' appear, as we saw, to glance significantly at Ex. 33.20; while twice in this context Jesus is described as the only begotten (14 and 18). We may claim therefore that here we have another passage to place beside the three mentioned above (II Cor. 3–4; Heb. 3; and the Transfiguration story) all of which deal with Moses, Jesus and glory, and two of which emphasize the sonship of our Lord.

'His face did shine as the sun', says Matt. 17.2; and with these words we may compare what is related of Moses.[2] Philo declares that when Moses descended from the mount 'those who saw him were filled with awe and amazement; nor even could their eyes continue to stand the dazzling brightness that flashed from him like the rays of the sun' (*Moses* II.70). It is interesting that Eusebius makes a direct comparison of the two incidents:

When Moses descended from the Mount, his face was seen full of glory: for it is written, 'And Moses descending from the Mount did not know that the appearance of the skin of his face was glorified while he spake to him. And Aaron and all the elders of Israel saw Moses, and the appearance of the skin of his face was glorified' (Ex. 34.29). In the same way, only more grandly, our Saviour led His disciples 'to

[1] In Wagenseil's *Tela Ignea Satanae* vol 2, Nizzachon Vetus occupies the first 260 pages, Hebrew and a Latin translation. The original Hebrew was taken 'ex Ms Bibliothecae Argentoratensis' (i.e. of Strasbourg). The passage quoted above comes from a comment on Ex. 34.33, and it gives the anonymous Jewish writer an occasion to claim that Moses was superior to Jesus. Though he shows some acquaintance with the Gospels, it is fragmentary and inexact. It is not impossible that some elements from the earliest times survive here and there in this document.

[2] A. M. Ramsey, *The Glory of God and the Transfiguration of Christ*, p. 120, shows how Matthew's account of the Transfiguration makes the connexion with Moses clearer, especially in the words 'his face did shine as the sun.' The skin of Moses' face shone, but 'here in contrast is the new and greater Moses, whose face shines not with a reflected glory but with the unborrowed glory as of the sun's own rays. Thus is the old covenant utterly surpassed by the new, "for if that which passeth away was with glory, how much more that which remaineth is in glory" (II Cor. 3.11).'

a very high mountain, and he was transfigured before them, and his face did shine as the sun, and his garments were white like the light.'[1]

The fear of the Israelites to approach Moses (Ex. 34.30) may throw some light on the attitude of the multitude towards Jesus when he descended from the mount: 'when they saw him, they were greatly amazed' (Mark 9.15).[2] And it is just possible that the reaction of those who came to arrest Jesus in John 18.6 reflects the same feature of Ex. 34.30. For in place of the Gethsemane prayer, which is not included in John's account, there is the prayer of John 17, full of references to glory. 'When Jesus had spoken these words' (18.1) he went out to the garden and the account of the arrest follows immediately, beginning with the discomfiture of those who approached him.

It will be remembered that the Transfiguration occurred *'after six days'* (Mark 9.2). Some have found here a connexion with Ex. 24.16. D. F. Strauss, for example, linked Ex. 24 and 34, since both passages deal with Moses' sojourn in the mount at the time of the law-giving; and, as at the Transfiguration, mention is made of three attendants (Ex. 24.9), a cloud (24.15 f.), entering into the cloud (24.18) and the voice out of the cloud (24.18), and as just mentioned the six days of 24.16.

It is a remarkable fact that it is possible to trace in the Fourth Gospel several periods of seven days and to find suggestions that Jesus manifested his glory 'after six days':

(*a*) The opening incidents of the Gospel deal with four successive days, 1.19, 29, 35, 43; then[3] chapter 2 begins, 'And the third day . . .' Joining these together we may infer that the wedding at Cana took place after six days, and it was then that 'he manifested his glory' (2.11).[4]

(*b*) In chapter 7 we have another week, corresponding to the

---

[1] *Demonstratio Evangelica* III.2, W. J. Ferrar's translation (p. 107 in vol. I of his edition: *The Proof of the Gospel*, 1920).

[2] Cf. the comment of V. Taylor on this verse (*The Gospel according to St Mark*, 1952).

[3] On the progressive unfolding of the revelation of Christ which these four days present, see my note in *Expository Times* 67 (May 1956), p. 245.

[4] The Jerusalem Bible points out that the Gospel begins with a complete week. Cf. B. W. Bacon: 'This self-revelation is described as occurring in a sequence of six days and culminates in the Miracle at Cana of Galilee on the seventh' ('After Six Days: a new clue for Gospel critics', *Harvard Theological Review* 8 [1915], pp. 94–121).

Feast of Tabernacles. And while some have contended that the last great day of verse 37 was the eighth, there is reason to believe that this was the seventh,[1] sometimes called the Great Hosanna. Here again it is after six days that Jesus manifests himself. If we remember to omit the pericope 7.53–8.11, the words of 8.12 follow on after the Tabernacles section of the previous chapter and should probably be taken as spoken on the seventh day; once more we have the glory of Christ, 'I am the light of the world' (and note the references to glory in the discussion following, 8.50, 54).

(*c*) There is a week also at the end of the Gospel. Six days are mentioned in 12.1, and it was at the end of this period that Jesus was crucified. In this Gospel, the Cross is the crowning glory of all (cf. 13.31; 12.23).

It seems significant that similar periods should be found at the beginning and end of the Gospel, and probably in the middle, too; and while I do not press this point, but rather offer it for consideration, it would confirm the view that John finds the manifestation of Christ's glory, not in a single event like the Transfiguration, but (at least for those with eyes to see) throughout his ministry and supremely in his Cross. 'We beheld his glory'; and as at the Transfiguration it was repeatedly 'after six days'.

Two eschatological features often found together are light and water (Rev. 22; Zech. 14); and it may be more than coincidence that in all the three places mentioned above there is not only the manifestation of Christ's glory, but also a reference to water. In (*a*) water is changed into wine; in (*b*) living water is offered in 7.37–38; and in (*c*) water and blood come from the side of the crucified.

The whole subject of the glory of Christ in this Gospel is of importance; the words 'glory' and 'glorify' occur more often than in any other Gospel, especially in references to Christ. We are not concerned with the theme in all its bearings, but one point, the association of glory with the Cross, warrants further reference as we close the present chapter. When Jesus says in 12.23, 'The hour is come, that the Son of man should be glorified', this is his

---

[1] So Lagrange, Loisy, R. H. Lightfoot; and J. Jeremias (*Golgotha*), H. Bornhäuser, *Sukkah*, p. 35, and E. G. King, *Yalkut on Zechariah*, p. 120.

response to the coming of the Greeks. Their request (12.21) reminded him of the price he must pay if he would draw men to himself (32 f.), and of the law of the grain of wheat which he must obey. Again in the same colloquy he says, 'Father, glorify thy name'; and the divine answer declares, 'I have both glorified it, and will glorify it again' (28).[1]

This association of glory with the Cross is found again in the following chapter; in 13.31–33 the word 'glory' or 'glorify' occurs five times, and it is precisely at the point where Judas goes out. 'When therefore he was gone out, Jesus saith, Now is the Son of man glorified. . . .' The 'night' (30) of Judas's treachery is the background for the glory of Christ's sacrifice.

In many places of the New Testament the glory of Christ is linked with his return 'in power and great glory'. But John in contrast shows that the glory of Christ is most marked at the point when with Judas's exit the wheels of the Passion Story begin to turn. It is sometimes said that John accepts the traditional eschatology, and this may be so; but he never associates glory with the return of Christ. It is in the event of the Passion that we are to see the glory of Christ, and the repetition of the word gives added emphasis.[2]

---

[1] E. A. Abbott thinks we are here concerned with 'a new Exodus from Egypt' and he maintains (not very convincingly) that 'the ruler of this world' (12.31) corresponds to Pharaoh. He points to the remarkable fact that *doxazo* does not occur in the LXX before the Song of Moses at the Red Sea (Ex. 15) and then it occurs five times and the adverb 'gloriously' twice. 'So here, the Son in prospect of the second Exodus, exclaimed to the Father, "Father, glorify they name" and receives the reply, "I have both glorified it and will glorify it again" (*Diatessarica* 10.iii, p. 456).

[2] Cf. Dodd, pp. 373 ff.

X

THE FAREWELL DISCOURSE AND PRAYER

AT the close of the life of Moses, as given in the Old Testament, there is a farewell discourse ending with a prayer for the tribes of Israel. The whole book of Deuteronomy may be regarded as a farewell discourse, for it was, according to 1.3, delivered in the fortieth year of the wilderness wanderings and the eleventh month. It ends with the blessing of the tribes (ch. 33).[1] From another point of view, the Song of Moses (ch. 32) corresponds to a farewell discourse, since various events have intervened in the earlier chapters, particularly the charge to Joshua (ch. 31).

Now, St John's Gospel ends the earthly ministry of Jesus with a farewell discourse and prayer (chs. 13–17), and several points of contact with Deuteronomy noted below are sufficient, I think, to establish a connexion of some kind.

One detail from the Targums may be mentioned at the outset, though this may be no more than a coincidence. Deut. 32 begins straight away with the words of Moses, 'Give ear, ye heavens . . .' But in the Jerusalem Targum I the section begins as follows: 'And when the last end of Moses the prophet was at hand, that he should be gathered from the world.' (The fragmentary Jerusalem Targum II has, 'When the end of Moses came, that he should be removed from the world.') With this may be compared the beginning of John 13.1, 'Jesus knowing that his hour was come that he should depart out of this world . . .'

Then follows the feet-washing; and this presents a curious parallel with a story about Moses which will be noticed in chapter XII. At present we are concerned with the discourse. One

---

[1] As A. Bentzen points out, farewell speeches are 'ascribed to several of Israel's great leaders before their death' (*Introduction to the Old Testament* Part I, pp. 206 f.). Cf. J. Munck, 'Discours d'adieu dans le Nouveau Testament et dans la littérature biblique', pp. 155–70 in the Goguel Festschrift, *Aux sources de la tradition chrétienne*. It has often been pointed out that the Johannine final discourse takes the place of the apocalyptic discourse in the other Gospels.

of its main themes is to be found in the recurring words, 'If ye love me ye will keep my commandments' (14.15; and cf. 14.21, 23; 15.10). This is also one of the recurring injunctions of Deuteronomy; see, for instance, 7.9, 'the faithful God which keepeth covenant and mercy with them that love him and keep his commandments', and cf. 5.10; 11.1 and 22; 13.3–4; 19.9; 30.16. Incidentally the expression 'to keep commandments', which occurs several times in John, is found in only one other place in the Gospels, Matt. 19.17, where the Marcan and Lucan parallels have a different phrase.

The message of John 14.1, 'Let not your heart be troubled', is also a recurring theme of Deuteronomy. A twofold form is given in 14.27, 'Let not your heart be troubled, neither let it be afraid'; and the injunction occurs in a similar twofold form several times in Deuteronomy: 'fear not, neither be dismayed' (31.8; cf. 1.21, 29; 7.18). Before we move on from John 14.1 it may be mentioned that Oesterley in his *Jewish Background of the Christian Liturgy* interprets the last discourse by means of the Passover service, and he connects John 14.1–2 with the promised land. This is not very convincing, although Ex. 23.30 does say: 'to bring thee into the *place* which I have *prepared*', thus giving a verbal parallel with the words, 'I go to prepare a place for you.'

We are on surer ground with the choosing of the disciples, especially when we remember that Jesus is ratifying a covenant with the New Israel which they represent. The relevant passages are John 15.16, 'Ye did not choose me, but I chose you', and verse 19, 'I chose you out of the world.' Once again we have a theme which is referred to in Deuteronomy again and again: 4.37; 7.6–7; 10.15; 14.2, and cf. 21.5 (of the priests). The expression in 7.6, 'the Lord thy God hath chosen thee . . . above all peoples that are upon the face of the earth,' should be literally '*out of* all peoples', as in RVm. Here we have something even closer to the words of John 15.19: 'I chose you *out of the world*.' Deut. 10.15 also reads 'out of all peoples', and again in 14.2, 'out of all peoples that are upon the face of the earth' (both passages as in RVm).

When we come to the word 'abide', which is so characteristic of this Upper Room Discourse, particularly in chapter 15, we might at first feel we are here dealing with a more mystical conception and that Old Testament roots are out of the question. And yet even here, the following emerges. Salkinson and Ginsburg in their Hebrew translation of the New Testament, render 'abide' in John 15 by the word *dabaq*, which usually means 'cleave to'. It is often used with the preposition 'b', which they include here in verses 4 and 7, so that *'menō en'* (Greek) becomes *'dabaq b'*. Now, this is a favourite term of Deuteronomy! Consider for example Deut. 10.20: 'Thou shalt fear the Lord thy God; him shalt thou serve; and to him thou shalt cleave.' Again Deut. 11.22, 'For if ye shall diligently keep all this commandment which I command you, to do it; to love the Lord your God, to walk in all his ways, and to cleave unto him.' This verse is especially interesting, as it not only contains the phrase 'cleave unto him' (which according to Salkinson and Ginsburg is equivalent to the Johannine 'abide in') but also two other Johannine phrases, 'keeping the commandment', and 'loving (the Lord)'. Deut. 13.4 also includes 'keep his commandments . . . and cleave unto him'; and in Deut. 30.20 we have the words, 'To love the Lord thy God, to obey his voice, and to cleave unto him: for he is thy life.' Two other passages usually ascribed to D may be mentioned: Josh. 22.5, 'to love the Lord your God . . . and to keep his commandments, and to cleave unto him'; and Josh. 23.8–11.

It thus appears that even a phrase like 'abide in' is not a mystical expression with Hellenistic affinities, but corresponds to a familiar Pentateuchal phrase. Salkinson and Ginsburg use *dabaq b* in John 15.4 of the branch abiding in the vine, as well as in the instances where the reference is directly to the believers' relation to the Lord. The Johannine idea of mutual indwelling does, of course, go beyond anything we find in Deuteronomy. At the same time the richer concept found in John may be based upon the Pentateuchal concept, a Christian expansion, as it were. Even in the Old Testament there is frequent reference to God dwelling among or in the midst of his people; the New Testament deepens this, making the union a much closer one. There is no doubt of the fact that the two ideas are related; Paul in II Cor. 6.16 says, 'we are a temple of the living God', and he continues immediately, 'even as God said, I will dwell in them, and walk in them' (Lev. 26.11–12).

When we come to the High Priestly Prayer of chapter 17 we

can trace a few points of contact with Deuteronomy, particularly
with chapters 32 f.: John 17.8 'words . . . I have given unto
them . . . they have received them'; Deut. 33.3 'everyone received of thy words.' The terms 'Holy Father' (John 17.11) and
'Righteous Father' (17.25) may be compared with Deut. 32.4,
'just and right is he'; the LXX reads *dikaios kai hosios* (righteous
and holy). Then with John 17.6, 'I manifested thy name unto the
men whom thou gavest me out of the world . . . they have kept
thy word', and 17.26, 'I made known unto them thy name', we
may compare Deut. 32.3, 'I will proclaim the name of the Lord',
and 33.9, 'they have observed thy word'.

Some authorities have connected the idea of making known the
name of God with various Hellenistic influences, but we should
notice how biblical the conception is; cf. Ex. 6.3, 'by my name
Jehovah I was not known to them'; the LXX, a Yemen manuscript of the eleventh century and the Targum of Onkelos have,
'my name Jehovah I made not known to them.'[1] Then in Ex.
33.19 we have the words, 'I will proclaim the name of the Lord
before thee.' Similarly the words of John 14.21, 'I will manifest
myself unto him' (ἐμφανίσω αὐτῷ ἐμαυτόν), and 14.22, 'thou wilt
manifest thyself unto us' (ἡμῖν μέλλεις ἐμφανίζειν σεαυτόν), find a
close parallel in Ex. 33.18, 'Show me thy glory', or as the LXX
puts it, 'Manifest thyself unto me' (ἐμφάνισόν μοι σεαυτόν).

Two points connecting with Moses traditions outside the Bible
may be mentioned, but I do not wish to rest anything upon them
and they may be only coincidences. (*a*) The pre-existence of which
John 17.24 speaks is different from that referred to in the *Assumption of Moses* 1.14, but there is one common phrase. *Ass. Mos.*:
'He prepared me before the foundation of the world, that I should
be the mediator of His covenant.' John 17.24: 'Thou lovedst me
before the foundation of the world.' Gelasius's quotation of this
passage of the *Assumption* shows that the three Greek words
involved are identical. (*b*) The other point comes from the story
that the angel of death approached Moses, who repulsed him, for
he had no claim on him. The angel (Samael) was unable to obtain
possession of his soul, and so Moses died by the kiss of God.[2]

---

[1] Supported also by the Vulgate and Syriac; see S. R. Driver on this
verse in his commentary on Exodus.
[2] Cf. *TWNT* IV, p. 858.

With this idea of having no claim on him we may compare John 14.30, 'for the prince of the world cometh: and he hath nothing in me.'

Another detail worth mentioning is that against the words of John 14.1, 'believe in God and believe in me', Nestle has a marginal reference to Ex. 14.31, 'they believed in the Lord and in his servant Moses.' In the same chapter of Exodus, which has several references to believing, the eighth verse says, 'If they will not believe thee, neither hearken to the voice of the first sign . . . they will believe the voice of the latter sign.' This inevitably reminds us of another passage in the same chapter of John, 14.11, 'Believe me . . . or else believe me for the very works' sake.' (It is, of course, obvious that the Johannine faith in Christ is a much deeper matter than the Israelites' belief in Moses, but the coincidence in phrasing is interesting. The latter kind of faith may be compared with the reference in the Dead Sea Scrolls to belief in the Teacher of Righteousness;[1] neither here nor in the case of Moses is the Christian connotation of a personal trust and committal implied.)

Looking back over the last few pages we can see that there are a number of striking coincidences, even in some of the main themes, between the final discourse and prayer of our Lord, and the book of Deuteronomy and a few other places of the Pentateuch. But we find most of the parallels in the final discourse and prayer of Moses as given in the book of Deuteronomy.[2]

---

[1] The Habakkuk Commentary (1Q pHab) 2.4: 'their faith in the teacher of righteousness'.

[2] It will be recalled that there is a direct reference to Deuteronomy elsewhere in John, in the passage concerning two witnesses, 8.17 (cf. Deut. 17.6 and 19.15). Our Lord's special regard for Deuteronomy may be seen in the fact that the replies to the three temptations, as given in Matt. and Luke, are all taken from this book (Deut. 8.3; 6.13 and 16).

XI

WHERE JOHANNINE = PENTATEUCHAL

In the last chapter we considered a number of parallels linking together the Upper Room Discourse and Prayer and corresponding passages in the Mosaic literature. There are similar parallels in other parts of St John, and in a sense all the chapters of the present work provide examples. But at this point we are to think of matters of vocabulary and phrase which have not emerged — previously in connexion with such outstanding subjects as water, bread and the rest.

It is well known that the language of the Fourth Gospel has its own distinctive flavour; there are expressions that we should immediately label as Johannine. Scholars have looked in various directions to trace the sources of language and theme behind this Gospel; and while the Torah of Moses has not been neglected by any means, it is doubtful if sufficient attention has been given to it, particularly in regard to matters of style and vocabulary.

Let us begin with a chapter which figured in the previous section, Ex. 4. The opening verse says, 'they will not believe me nor hearken unto my voice.' Now, unless we knew the words were being quoted from the Pentateuch we might search mentally for them in St John, as they have such a characteristic ring. For 'hearing the voice' see John 5.37; 10.3, 16, 27; 18.37. Again Ex. 4.8, quoted previously in connexion with John 14, appears to distinguish belief in Moses from belief in his signs, and with this we may compare (in addition to John 14.11 cited earlier) John 10.38, 'though ye believe not me, believe the works.'

Once again consider the terms of Num. 16.28:

And Moses said, Hereby ye shall know that the Lord hath sent me to do all these works for I have not done them of my own mind (LXX, not of myself).

Here there is a whole cluster of terms which, like the atmosphere of the sentence, we might call Johannine: *know, sent me, do these works, not of myself.* The following are relevant: John 13.35, 'by this shall all men know'; 8.28, 'then you will know'; 5.30, 'I do nothing of myself'; 7.28, 'I have not come of myself but he is true who sent me'; 8.42, 'I have not come of myself but he sent me'; 14.10, 'I speak not of myself . . . the Father doeth his works.' 'Doing works' occurs repeatedly, 5.36 (twice); 7.3; 10.25, 37; 15.24; 17.4. If one looks up the word 'sent' in a concordance he will find many cases where the word is used of Moses, and he will wonder if some of the involved and circuitous explanations of the Johannine 'sent one' have not missed a source which lies much closer at hand.

The entire conception of a prophet like unto Moses, Deut. 18.15 ff., is basic to the understanding of St John and there is no need to emphasize this further here; but at the moment we are thinking of various expressions and phrases associated with it. In Deut. 18 the prophet is to speak in the name of the Lord (v. 19); God's words are put in his mouth and 'he shall speak unto them all that I shall command him' (v. 18). In this connexion we may recall a few Johannine passages:

5.43, 'I am come in my Father's name';
8.28, 'as the Father taught me, I speak these things';
7.16, 'My teaching is not mine, but his that sent me';
12.49, 'For I spake not from myself; but the Father which sent me, he hath given me a commandment, what I should say, and what I should speak' (cf. 17.8).

An interesting parallel may be traced in John 5.19 f., where it is said that the Son does (*poieō*) what he sees the Father doing, and the Father shows (*deiknumi*) him all (*panta*) that he does. In Ex. 25.9 Moses makes (*poieō*) the Tabernacle according to all (*panta*) that God shows (*deiknuō*) him. Cf. Ex. 25.40, quoted in Heb. 8 in a Moses/Christ passage; see also Ex. 26.30; 27.8; Num. 8.4.

The 'going out and coming in' of John 10 may be compared with the similar expressions in Num. 27.17; it will be observed that the shepherd imagery occurs in both passages. A successor to Moses is being sought 'which may go out before them, and which may come in before them, and which may lead them out and which may bring them in; that the congregation of the Lord be not as sheep which have no shepherd'; cf. 27.21, 'at his word shall they go out, and at his word they shall come in.' Here there are several ideas and expressions comparable with John 10. The whole passage Num. 27.15–23 is an important one and will come up again in later chapters. We shall see that the thought of Moses as a shepherd was later amplified; and we shall suggest, too, that the action of Moses in 'putting his honour upon' Joshua, or 'giving him his glory', is not unrelated to the action of Jesus in giving his glory to his disciples (John 17.22).

One or two other examples of this surprising relationship between Johannine and Pentateuchal language may be briefly mentioned. (*a*) Num. 14.11: 'And the Lord said unto Moses, How long will this people despise me? and how long will they not believe in me, for all the signs which I have wrought among them?' The RVm very appropriately gives a cross-reference to John 12.37: 'But though he had done so many signs before them, yet they believed not on him.' (*b*) Ex. 3.12–15 is interesting with its mention of Moses as 'sent', the token or sign, and the 'name' of God, (*c*) Deut. 18.21 with its question 'How shall we know?' following the passage about the prophet like Moses, and (*d*) Deut. 9.11 and 10.4 declaring that the law was 'given' (i.e. through Moses); cf. John 1.17. (*e*) C. H. Dodd draws attention to the fact that John 7.24, 'judge righteous judgment', recalls Deut. 16.18, where the same expression occurs (p. 79).[1]

---

[1] The examples given in the foregoing and in the other chapters were drawn up before I met with Dr A. Guilding's book *The Fourth Gospel and Jewish Worship* (1960) and I see that some instances are common ground. I do not, however, find her main thesis convincing that the material of the Fourth Gospel is arranged according to a Jewish three-year lectionary scheme.

XII

MOSES AND HIS SUCCESSOR JOSHUA

WHEN one begins to notice the numerous connecting links between Jesus and Moses in the Fourth Gospel, it perhaps never occurs to us that such an incident as the feet-washing (John 13) might be brought into this context. However, it is a striking fact that Jewish legends in amplifying the story in Num. 27.15–23 describe the way in which Moses acted as a servant to Joshua, the roles being exchanged. In one account it is said that Moses prepared a basin of water.[1]

This detail may be a mere coincidence, but there are other points of connexion. Num. 27.20 says: 'thou shalt put of thine honour upon him'; and the Hebrew word for 'put' is 'give'. With this compare John 17.22: 'and the glory which thou hast given me I have given unto them.' If we insist on the word 'glory' we may find it in the LXX of Num. 27.20, where both 'give' and 'glory' are to be found.

As we saw earlier, there are a number of links between the glory of Moses and of Christ; and now it may be added that just as Moses conveyed, as it were, his glory to Joshua so Jesus did the same to his disciples. And as Moses exchanged the usual roles and acted on this one occasion at the end of his life as Joshua's attendant, so Jesus did the same to his disciples.

I do not wish to press the point about the basin of water, as this particular detail is of late occurrence.[2] But there is ample evidence for the stories about Moses serving Joshua, and this

---

[1] Cf. A. Wünsche, *Aus Israels Lehrhallen: Kleine Midraschim* I (1907), pp. 148–50.

[2] F. B. Meyer connects the feet-washing with the laver in the temple court. The priests washed there before being consecrated for their work in the Holy Place (Ex. 29.4; Lev. 16.4); cf. Heb. 10.22, where Christians are bidden to draw near, their bodies washed with pure water. 'In this scene . . . John 13 . . . we find the spiritual counterpart of the Laver, and in the following chapters we stand in the Presence-Chamber' (*Love to the Uttermost*, chapters on John 13–21, a sequel to *Life and Light of Men*).

general picture is likely to be very much earlier than some of the more detailed accounts, because the whole conception is derived from Num. 27, where Moses gives his glory and honour to Joshua. The Midrash Rabba on Deut. 9.9 in referring to the same theme describes how Moses walked on the left of Joshua; this implies that their usual roles were reversed, Moses taking the disciple's place. The anxiety of some Rabbinic writings to show that when Moses imparted his glory to his successor it did not involve any diminution in his own glory may be explained as a reaction against the stories of Moses serving Joshua. If this is the true explanation, it confirms the antiquity of the stories. Midrash Siphre on Numbers[1] says in this connexion that the glory of Moses was like the sun, while that of Joshua was like the moon.

Some may wonder how the question of the historicity of John 13 is affected by the parallel noted. In answer to this it may be pointed out that the Evangelist is not necessarily inventing incidents to correspond with the Mosaic tradition; he rather selects those happenings which belong to this scheme. Moreover, it is probable that the Moses/Christ parallelism did not originate with the early Church, but goes back to our Lord himself and to the way in which he regarded and interpreted his mission. The Moses motif is, of course, only one of several strands, but it seems that its place has not been sufficiently recognized.

It is remarkable that the passage of Numbers which connects with John 13 and 17, as shown above, is precisely the passage to which we were led in the previous chapter in considering John 10; Num. 27.17 speaks of the sheep and of the shepherd leading them out and bringing them in.

Again it is in the charge to *Joshua* in Deut. 31.7–8 that we find the words 'fear not, neither be dismayed'. And so the final charge of Jesus to his disciples includes the injunction, 'Let not your heart be troubled, neither let it be fearful' (14.27, cf. 14.1). The LXX rendering of Deut. 31.8 has μὴ φοβοῦ, μηδὲ δειλία: cf. John 14.27 μηδὲ δειλιάτω.

According to Deut. 34.9, Moses apparently imparted the Spirit to Joshua and ordained him to his responsible office: 'And Joshua

[1] Cf. H. G. Horovitz, *Corpus Tannaiticum*, 1917, Abteilung 3, Teil 3, Fasc. 1; p. 187; also p. 321. Cf. also Baba Bathra 75a.

the son of Nun was full of the spirit of wisdom; for Moses had laid his hands upon him: and the children of Israel hearkened unto him, and did as the Lord commanded Moses.' The Rabbis regarded this incident as vital for the whole idea of succession. All ordinations looked back to this one.[1]

C. K. Barrett points out that in John 15.16 ('I have chosen you and ordained you'), the word translated 'ordained', *ethēka*, may be a rendering or echo of the Hebrew *samak*, which has among its meaning 'to lay the hands on (the head of), that is to ordain'; the word is commonly used of the ordination of a scholar as Rabbi. It is also, one might add, the word used in Deut. 34.9 of Moses laying his hands upon Joshua. There is, of course, no record that Jesus ever laid his hands on his disciples[2] and instead we find that the Spirit is imparted by sufflation (John 20.22) with an obvious reference to Gen. 2.7. Thus, while in some matters Christ may be related to his disciples as Moses was to Joshua, in others it is as the Creator to the man he has made.

In some of the sayings of Jesus in John 13–21, the disciples are representatives of the whole Church; thus all Christians have without question taken for themselves such a section as 14.1–3. Others are addressed to the apostles as such (15.27), others to the apostles as representatives of the Christian ministry.[3] And in the final chapter there are special sayings relating to Peter.

In regard to the last point we may observe that just as Moses when leaving the world appointed Joshua as shepherd (Num. 27.16–18) so Jesus appoints Peter as shepherd (John 21). According to Aboth R. Nathan 17, Moses said to Joshua, 'This people which I commit to you, I commit to you only as kids and lambs, as frail children'.[4] Similarly Jesus says to Peter, 'Feed my lambs'

---

[1] D. Daube translates as follows the Siphre comment on Num. 27.23, where Moses lays his hands upon Joshua: 'He pressed on him as one presses on a vessel already full to overflowing (Joshua having been endowed with the Spirit even before his ordination—27.18) in order to stuff even more into it.' He adds, 'Since for the Siphre Joshua's appointment is simply the first Rabbinic ordination on which all further ones are modelled, it is plain that the rite of *samakh*, by this time, has lost nothing of its specific character' (*New Testament and Rabbinic Judaism*, p. 232).

[2] Daube (*op. cit.*) suggests a reason for this.

[3] Cf. H. C. G. Moule, *Outlines of Christian Doctrine* (1889), pp. 219 f.

[4] S.-B. 2, p. 587; reference is made also to the Midrash Rabbah on Song of Songs 1.8, where a similar passage occurs.

(21.15). Eusebius in the course of an extended comparison of Christ and Moses regards Peter as answering to Joshua: 'Moses changed the name of Nave to Jesus, and likewise the Saviour changed that of Simon to Peter.'[1]

The points touched on in this chapter may be summarized as follows:

(*a*) Moses at the time of handing over his authority to Joshua served him. This is not stated in the Old Testament, but is well authenticated in later tradition.

(*b*) Moses 'gave' his glory to Joshua (Num. 27.20).

(*c*) Moses imparted the Spirit to Joshua and 'ordained' him (Deut. 34.9).

(*d*) Joshua was called to be a shepherd as Moses had been (Num. 27.17). Matters of comparison have been found in the later chapters of John answering to these:

(*a*) Jesus fulfilled the office of a servant in relation to his disciples (13.1 ff.).

(*b*) Jesus gave his glory to his disciples (17.22).

(*c*) Jesus imparted the Spirit to his disciples (20.22); and to quote the words of 15.16, 'I chose you and appointed you', or, as some would suggest, 'ordained you'.

(*d*) Peter as the leading disciple is called to tend the sheep (21.15–17) as Jesus had done (ch. 10).[2] As we have seen, there is the coincidence, and it may be no more, that both Joshua (at least in later tradition) and Peter were told to be mindful of the lambs. Without relying upon the points which emerge only in later sources, I think we can claim that the parallels are sufficiently striking to be significant.

[1] *Demonstratio Evangelica* III.2; W. J. Ferrar's translation, vol. I, p. 107.
[2] This is stressed by Bishop Cassian in the article referred to on p. 44 ('John xxi', *New Testament Studies* 3 [Jan. 1957], pp. 132–6).

XIII

CHRIST AND THE TORAH

SINCE the term 'Moses' extends beyond the person of the Hebrew leader and embraces the five books often designated by his name, as in the phrase 'Moses and the prophets', our subject should include the contrast drawn out in the Fourth Gospel between Christ and the Torah. The law-giving of Ex. 20 is an important part of the wilderness narrative; so we are not unduly widening our theme. This contrast is, of course, indicated in the opening chapter: 'For the law was given by Moses; grace and truth came by Jesus Christ' (1.17); and the thought of this verse is one of the recurring themes of the whole Gospel. This is shown by the way in which the Evangelist takes designations and descriptions of the Torah and applies them to Jesus. Consider the following in reference to the terms Life, Light, Bread and Water:

(*a*) 'The words of Torah are the life of this age and the life of the age to come' (Pesiqta 102b).

(*b*) In regard to light, an example may be taken from the Midrash Siphre on Num. 6 in a comment on the words, 'the Lord make his face to shine upon thee'; this, it is said, is the light of the Torah. Prov. 6.23 is adduced in illustration, with the statement that the commandment is a lamp and the Torah is light.

(*c*) Again Pesiqta 80b thus explains Prov. 25.21: If thine enemy hunger, feed him with bread, that is with the bread of Torah.

(*d*) There are many examples of the imagery of water; and the comment of Siphre on Deut. 11.22 is typical of a large number. 'As water is life for the world, so also the words of Torah are life for the world.'

It will be observed that these are among the most familiar conceptions of the Fourth Gospel; it is in Jesus that life and light are to be found; he himself is the Bread, and from him proceed the living waters.[1]

[1] The Christ/Torah background of these statements is widely recognized, as in the commentaries of Hoskyns, Barrett and others; see also Dodd, pp. 75–86.

This contrast is especially important in connexion with the Prologue. J. Rendel Harris showed in an impressive and convincing way that statements which had been made about Wisdom are here transferred to the Christ-Logos (*The Origin of the Prologue to St John's Gospel*, 1917); but later scholars have contended that it was because Wisdom had been identified with the Torah that the Prologue had developed this theme.[1]

There is, of course, a real Christological interest in the Prologue; and we know from other parts of the New Testament that the early Christians found the conception of Wisdom (in Prov. 8 and in the post-canonical developments branching from it) particularly useful in interpreting the person of Christ. This is clear from such passages as I Cor. 1.24, the great hymn of Col. 1.15–20 and Heb. 1.3, the language of which passage is derived from the description of Wisdom in Wisd. 7.26. Most of the statements made about the Logos in John 1 had been made concerning Wisdom. She was in the beginning (Prov. 8.22); she was the agent in creation (Prov. 3.19; 8.30;[2] Wisd. 7.22); she tabernacled among men, at least 'in Jacob', the people of Israel (Ecclus. 24.8).[3] But at the same time it is vital to remember that the Jews had identified Wisdom with the Torah, and one of the main concerns of the Prologue is to show that the Wisdom or Word of God is to be recognized in Christ and not in the Jewish Law.

One of the sapiential passages drawn upon in the Prologue is Ecclus. 24; and in the closing parts of this eloquent description of the divine Wisdom it is clear that the identification with the Torah is already established:

All these things are the book of the covenant of God Most High, the Law which Moses commanded as a heritage for the assemblies of Jacob (24.23).

The identification is clear also in 1 Baruch 3.9–4.4. In later Rabbinic writings it becomes an established doctrine. It was in this way that the pre-existence of the Torah and its part in the creation came to be affirmed. The Jerusalem Targum had even substituted the word 'wisdom' for 'beginning' in its paraphrase of Gen. 1.1,

---

[1] Cf. G. Kittel in *TWNT* IV, pp. 138 ff.

[2] If 'master-workman' be accepted as the meaning of the Hebrew *'amon*.

[3] For other examples see Harris, *op. cit.*, and Dodd, pp. 274 f.

on the strength of their apparent equivalence in Prov. 8.22.[1]

It is in the light of these extravagant claims made for the Torah (on the basis of its identification with Wisdom) that the Prologue should be interpreted; Christ, it is affirmed, is the true Wisdom or Logos, and it was through him that all things were made (1.3). It is he who is 'the light of men' (1.4); even the extended description of 1.9, 'the light that lighteth every man', may be found in Jewish writings in reference to the Torah—'the light of the law which was given to lighten every man' (*Test. Levi* 14.4).[2] And if the Logos-Son was in the bosom of the Father (1.18), so according to Jewish conceptions was the Torah: 'Before the world was made the Torah was written and lay in the bosom of God.'[3]

We thus have in the Prologue a transference to Christ of what had been ascribed to the Torah. This is indeed one of the ruling motifs of the Gospel as a whole. In earlier chapters a number of examples have been mentioned, and in passing these under review some further points may be mentioned here, some of which bring out in various ways the Christ-Torah contrast.

In the story of the miracle at Cana the water-pots are described as 'set there after the Jews' manner of purifying' (2.6), so that in a sense they symbolize the external cleansing prescribed in the Law, as contrasted with the festive wine brought by Jesus. Wine itself in Rabbinic teaching symbolized the Torah, and so the whole story suggests that the true wine is the gift of Jesus. Exodus R. 25.7 quotes the words of Wisdom in Prov. 9.5, 'drink of the wine which I have mingled' and equates this wine with the Torah. There is also probably a suggestion, in the saying 'thou hast kept the good wine until now' (2.10), that the inferior wine corresponds to Judaism and the good wine to Christianity, which follows Judaism in time and comes at the climax of the ages. (Cf. Dodd, pp. 84 and 299.)

---

[1] Cf. R. Bultmann in *Eucharisterion* (Gunkel Festschrift, 1923), Part II, p. 12. See also the Mishnah tractate Aboth 3.15, where the Torah is 'the precious instrument by which the world was created' (Danby, p. 452).

[2] Cf. *Zeitschrift für neutestamentliche Wissenschaft* 49 (1958), pp. 288 ff.

[3] Attributed to Rabbi R. Eliezer ben Jose (2nd century AD) and quoted in Aboth of Rabbi Nathan; Prov. 8.30 is cited and evidently the alternative translation 'nursling' is being followed here for the Hebrew *'amon*. Cf. Dodd, p. 86.

Just as the water-pots of chapter 2 are set 'after the Jews' manner of purifying', so there may be point in the description of the well at Sychar as 'Jacob's well'; it belonged to the old régime and stands in contrast to the living water which Jesus offers. Christianity is an inner life; it resembles not a static receptacle to which men come but a living spring within. This inwardness (as shown in the context, 4.20–26) makes the spiritual life independent of places and temples; it is no longer a question of this mountain or that, but the hour has now come when worship is in spirit and truth. Moreover the old national boundaries are transcended, and the Samaritans as well as the Jews may find in Christ 'the Saviour of the world' (4.42).

The importance of the well imagery was noted earlier in chapter 7. The pool of Bethzatha (or whatever the name may have been) with its five porches (5.1 ff.) and the pool of Siloam (9.7) are not exactly wells, but they sustain the interest in water which is such a marked feature of these early chapters. Some have found in the five porches (5.2) a veiled reference to the Pentateuch! This is hardly likely, but one cannot rule it out as impossible. After all, the remains are still in existence and it may be that the original building was designed to symbolize the five books of the Torah. Augustine, however, was quite confident about the significance of this point in the story. 'Moses', he declares,

wrote five books, but in the five porches round the pool, sick men were lying, but they could not be healed. . . . For in those five porches, a figure of the five books, sick men were given over rather than made whole (*Exposition of Psalms* 70.20).

Again in a comment on Ps. 83.7 he writes, 'He who was not healed by the Law, that is in the porches, is healed by grace, through faith in the passion of our Lord Jesus Christ.' Archbishop Trench in his famous book on the miracles puts the matter in a somewhat guarded way:

Augustine, ever watching to bring out his great truth that the Law was for the revealing of sin, and could not effect its removal . . . finds a type, or at least an apt illustration of this, in those five porches, which showed their sick, but could not cure them.[1]

In the closing part of the same chapter (John 5.39–47) the

[1] 13th ed., 1886, p. 279.

matter of the Torah emerges quite plainly. This important passage shows that the Pharisees search their scriptures and yet fail to see that it is to Jesus that they bear witness. 'For if ye believed Moses, ye would believe me; for he wrote of me' (5.46). The very word Midrash (from *darash*, to search) may be hinted at here in the charge, 'Ye search the scriptures because ye think that in them ye have eternal life; and these are they which bear witness of me; and ye will not come to me, that ye may have life.' (39 f.). Life is to be found in him, and not in their searching of the Torah; the latter is only of use if it leads on to him. If they remain short of this climax, then the Law will merely accuse and convict them; and Moses in whom they trust will be their accuser (45). It is interesting to notice how this passage harmonizes with one of the main themes of St Paul, that the Law cannot save but rather awakens men to a sense of need in convicting them, showing their need of Christ. As the words of 7.19 put it, 'none of you keeps the law.'

The sixth chapter of John shows that the true bread of life is Jesus himself, not the Torah as the Jews alleged. The imagery of bread has been sufficiently dealt with in earlier pages; but something may be added here on the word 'true': 'my Father giveth you the true bread out of heaven' (6.32). This is a term which, of course, recurs throughout the Gospel, but it may be dwelt upon at this point, since 'true bread' provides a typical instance. The word ἀληθινός reminds us of the usage of Hebrews, where Judaism is the shadow and Christianity the substance. Behind both writings there lies, no doubt, the Platonic conception of the phenomenal world and the noumenal (or real, true) world.[1] Even St Paul in Col. 2.17 speaks of the Law, just as Hebrews does, as a 'shadow of the things to come'. In the Fourth Gospel this kind of comparison is brought out by means of the term 'true'. The word occurs only once in the Synoptic Gospels (Luke 16.11); once in St Paul, I Thess. 1.9; three times in Hebrews, and no less than nine times in St John's Gospel; if we add the four occurrences in I John and the ten in Revelation, we reach twenty-three

---

[1] In this connexion J. B. Lightfoot aptly quotes from Wordsworth:
The swan on still St Mary's lake
Floats double, swan and shadow.
See *Colossians* (1879), p. 267.

as the total in the Johannine writings. In John 6.32 the true bread found in Christ is contrasted with the manna of Judaism; in 15.1 the true vine is probably to be seen as over against the vine of Israel (cf. Ps. 80.8 ff. and Jer. 2.21). In 1.9 the true light is, in the immediate context, contrasted with John the Baptist (cf. 5.35), but there is also a tacit allusion to the light of the Torah. In 4.23 the true worshippers worship in spirit and truth, as contrasted with those who depend upon special mountains and particular places. Thus the word 'true' illustrates the contrast between Christ and the Law of Moses which runs through the Gospel.

Chapters 7 and 8 have been dealt with in connexion with the Rock and the Light; but one or two further points may be mentioned here. The statement in 7.22 that circumcision 'is not of Moses, but of the fathers', reminds one of St Paul's habit of going back beyond Moses to Abraham and the other patriarchs. Later in the same chapter (7.49) we have the Pharisees' disparaging reference to the accursed multitude 'which knoweth not the law'; these are the people who hang upon the words of Jesus. Once again the contrast between Jesus and the Torah is brought out, this time from a somewhat different angle. It is rather curious that the Pericope Adulterae, 7.53 to 8.11, though an alien intrusion, gives a perfect illustration of the contrast. 'In the law Moses commanded us to stone such' (8.5); but with Jesus were found grace and truth, 'Neither do I condemn thee; go thy way; from henceforth sin no more' (8.11). Can it be that the scribe who erroneously inserted this story here, probably a piece of floating tradition, was aware how well it illustrated one of the dominant themes of this Gospel?

In chapter 9 pointed reference is made to those who claim to be 'disciples of Moses' withdrawing themselves decisively from Jesus and from the blind man restored by him. Again it is a question of Moses or Christ: 'Thou art his disciple; but we are disciples of Moses. We know that God hath spoken unto Moses: but as for this man, we know not whence he is' (28 f.). The whole chapter also illustrates the theme of light and shows where the true 'light of the world' (9.5) is to be found. 'Life' is perhaps the ruling conception of chapters 10 and 11 which bring us almost to the end of the narrative of the ministry.

A small point from the Passion narrative may be mentioned.

When the Jews cry to Pilate, 'We have a law, and by that law he ought to die' (19.7) the reference may be to a specific law against blasphemy. But may there not also be a further suggestion of the incompatibility between Christ and Torah? Just as in the Prologue the Logos-Christ takes the place of the Torah, so at the end of the story the same alternatives stand out.

It is noticeable that when addressing the Jews Jesus speaks of 'your law' (8.17; 10.34). Again in the Upper Room discourse he says to his disciples, 'it is written in their law' (15.25). This does not by any means indicate that the Gospel was written by a Gentile.[1] Nor does it mean that the divine origin of the Law is being denied. Rather, because of their misuse of it it had become 'their law' since they made of it a final instrument of salvation, instead of seeing it as preparatory to Jesus and as witnessing to him.[2] (Cf. II Cor. 3.14–16, 'whensoever Moses is read, a veil lieth upon their heart'.) In his comment on John 8.17 Barrett says:

As at 7.19 . . . John indicates the rift that had opened between Synagogue and Church, and also his intention to fasten upon the Jews the witness, disregarded by them, of their own Scriptures. Also 'Jesus stands in the same relation to the Torah as his Father' (Odeberg).

There can be no possible doubt that the Evangelist looked upon the Torah as genuine divine revelation.

Some reference should be made, before we leave this subject, to the conception of a new Torah. This idea is more apparent in St Matthew than in St John, especially in the Sermon on the Mount, where the contrast with the law of Moses is brought out repeatedly. Also the clearly defined five discourses of St Matthew are no doubt intended to answer in some way to the five books of the Mosaic law. In St John the passage in chapter 13 which speaks of a 'new commandment' (vv. 34 f.) should perhaps be understood in a similar way.

Some authorities deny that the Jews expected a new law to be brought by the Messiah, and in support of this denial they quote Deut. R. 8.6:

Moses said to them (the Israelites), 'Lest you should say, "Another

[1] As H. M. Teeple maintains, *Novum Testamentum* 4 (Oct. 1960), p. 24.
[2] See Gutbrod, νόμος, *TWNT* IV, p. 1077.

Moses is to arise and to bring us another law from heaven", I make known to you at once that it is not in heaven; there is none of it left in heaven.'

(Cf. Deut. 30.11 f.) But this passage may well be anti-Christian polemic; in that case it would seem that some of the Rabbis at least abandoned the conception of a new Torah under the Messiah which had been taught earlier, abandoned it because of the use Christians made of it.

J. Klausner, the Jewish scholar, in his book *From Jesus to Paul* (1944), gives several Rabbinic references to the abrogation of the law in the time to come (p. 496). But this negative idea can be supplemented by means of other evidence of a more positive kind. It is true that references to a 'new Torah'[1] may at times mean a new interpretation of the one and only Torah, and W. D. Davies summarizes thus the general Rabbinic interpretation:

When the Rabbis taught . . . that the Messiah when he came would bring a new Law, they thought of that Law as new not in the sense that it would be contrary to the Law of Moses but that it would explain it more fully (*Paul and Rabbinic Judaism*, p. 72).

But the words of Eccles. R.11.8 seem to carry us beyond this: 'The Torah which a man learns in this world is vanity in comparison with the Torah which will be learnt in the days of the Messiah.'

The New Testament references to a law of Christ, as found (with varying phraseology) in both Gospels and Epistles, should be considered in the light of this Jewish expectation. In John there is in particular the 'new commandment' of 13.34 f. already mentioned. Also Christ's 'commandments' in the Upper Room discourse (14.15, 21; 15.10) may be brought within the same context of thought.

It is remarkable that while in the Synoptic Gospels there is a wealth of ethical teaching, there is none at all in St John throughout the public ministry, not a word on the love of one's neighbour for example. The law of love in St John is first found in the Upper Room, and is addressed to disciples. There is no doubt a special reason for this. In chapters 1–12, which deal with the public ministry, there is much about *believing* on Christ; in 13 onwards

[1] Cf. S.B. 4, pp. 1 f.

there is much about *love*—the section begins with the words: 'having loved his own . . . he loved them to the uttermost, or to the end.' It is when men have first come to Christ in faith and have received him that they are ready for instruction in righteousness. To begin with moral rules is not only futile, but may establish a new legalism instead of the realm of grace and truth. It may be that John is consciously countering this danger. That the danger was a real one may be seen in the Didachē and other early Christian writings.

St John's order is thus the same as that found in St Paul, who usually devotes the former part of his letters to expositions of grace and faith, while the instruction in righteousness comes normally towards the end (Romans, Ephesians, Galatians).

The idea of a new law has its dangers, and it is significant that in St John it is not prominent.[1] In the Prologue over against 'the law of Moses' stand grace and truth. It is the person of the Logos which holds the central place.

[1] On νόμος in the Fourth Gospel see *TWNT* IV, pp. 1075–7. This article is available in English in the Bible Key Words series, *Law*, by Kleinknecht and Gutbrod; see pp. 129–34.

XIV

THE SHEPHERD AND THE LAMB OF GOD

The Shepherd

Mention has already been made of the fact that Moses was a shepherd of God's people, and that in some places of the New Testament references to Christ as Shepherd reflect the influence of the Moses/Christ parallelism. The subject is referred to again here to give the matter specific mention in its own right, as it were; and to add one or two further details.

In chapter II attention was drawn to the wording of Heb. 13.20, where 'the great shepherd of the sheep' is described in language clearly derived from Isa. 63.11 with its distinct delineation of Moses as shepherd. The shepherd imagery of Num. 27.17 ff. was dealt with in chapter XI and XII, and it was seen that Moses 'went in and out' so that the community was not as a flock without a shepherd; and as Moses when leaving the world appointed Joshua as shepherd, so Jesus appoints Peter to the same office.

The ministry of Moses as shepherd was lovingly dwelt upon by the Jewish people.[1] Within the Old Testament mention may be made of Ps. 77.20, 'Thou leddest thy people like a flock, by the hand of Moses and Aaron.' In traditions outside the Bible the Midrash R. on Ex. 2.2 is important; here it is said that Moses was first tested as a shepherd of sheep before being allowed to act as shepherd of God's people. (A similar point is made by Philo in *Moses* I.60–62.) This Midrash passage depicts a kid which ran away; Moses followed it and found it drinking from a fountain.

When the kid had finished drinking Moses took it up with great tenderness and put it on his shoulder and carried it all the way back to the flock . . . and this thing that Moses did was very pleasing in the sight of God, and he said to Moses: 'How great are your tender

---

[1] Ginzberg's *Legends of the Jews* has a section on 'Moses as Faithful Shepherd', vol. 2 (1910), pp. 300 ff.; see also p. 316 and vol. 3, p. 51.

mercies; you took pity on the kid, because you are full of mercy; therefore you shall lead my people Israel and be their shepherd.'[1]

One cannot help being reminded of Luke 15.3–7 as well as of the Good Shepherd of John 10.

The passage about 'one shepherd' in Eccles. 12.11 is applied to Moses in the Midrash R. on Num. 14.4. There are also various Rabbinic references to Moses, Aaron and Miriam as the three shepherds. More important, Moses is thought of as the eschatological shepherd and is told, 'thou shalt lead them in the future world' (cf. Rev. 7.17).

One tradition emphasized the fact that Moses did not lose a single sheep. With this we may compare John 10.28 f.; 17.12, 'I guarded them and not one of them perished'; and 18.9.

The Lamb

It does not seem that much attention has been given to the fact that Moses in one tradition is compared to a lamb. According to the Jerusalem Targum on Ex. 1.15 Pharaoh dreamed of a pair of scales; on one scale of the balance was the land of Egypt, and on the other a lamb. The lamb proved to be the heavier. Pharaoh called in the magicians Jannes and Jambres, who gave as the interpretation the following message: A son shall be born in the community of Israel who will destroy all Egypt. Pharaoh's order concerning the slaying of the Hebrew male children arose from this dream. The same tradition is given in various other sources.[2] This association of Moses with the lamb concept may not throw much light on John 1.29 or any other passage of the Fourth Gospel; but it may be relevant in connexion with Revelation, where the Lamb, like Moses, opposes and overcomes the enemy of God. Cf. Rev. 15.3 with its reference to 'the song of Moses . . . and the song of the Lamb'. At the same time it may be recalled that attempts have been made to find in John 1.29 traces of the apocalyptic horned lamb, the bell-wether of God's flock who is

[1] As in I. B. Levner's *The Legends of Israel* (trans. J. Snowman), 1956, p. 28.
[2] See the article by Renée Bloch in *Recherches de Science Religieuse* 43 (1955), pp. 194–227.

destined to overcome the powers of evil and in that sense to take away the sin of the world.[1] Barrett[2] makes the point that John the Baptist may have referred to Jesus, or to the Coming One, as the apocalyptic Lamb; and the Church, while adopting the term from the Baptist, interpreted it in the light of the Passover Lamb; the Evangelist in his characteristic fashion combined more than one meaning in his use of the term.

It should be noted that it is possible to regard John 1.29 as making two propositions about Jesus: (*a*) He is the Lamb of God. (*b*) He is the One who takes away the sin of the world. This is well brought out in the Latin Vulgate by the repetition of the word 'Behold' (Ecce Agnus Dei, ecce qui tollit peccatum mundi). The words of (*b*) have no necessary connexion with the Lamb imagery and could be linked up with the wider context. The phrase of John 1.14, 'full of grace and truth', may reflect Ex. 34.6, 'plenteous in mercy and truth'; and it is at least interesting to observe that the very next verse in Ex. 34 says that God 'takes away (Heb. *nasa*') iniquity and transgression and sin'. Like the one disclosed in Ex. 34, the Christ of God is full of mercy and truth, and he takes away sin. Delitzsch's translation of John 1.29 (*nasa* '*awon*) has the exact phrase of Ex. 34.7.

There is wide support for the view that Passover associations are to be seen in the word 'Lamb', and this connects not only with other New Testament writings (I Cor. 5.7; I Peter 1.18 f.), but with other Johannine allusions, especially 19.36 (cf. Ex. 12.46 and Num. 9.12) and the hyssop of 19.29 (Ex. 12.22). It is often contended that John changed the date of the Crucifixion from that given in the other Gospels in order to bring out the fact that Jesus was the true Paschal Lamb, slain on the day and at the very time the Passover lambs were slain in the Temple.[3]

Another Passover allusion has been seen by some writers in John 13.1. Rendel Harris[4] drew attention to the words of Philo describing the allegorical meaning of the Exodus: 'The Passover is the migration (διάβασις) of the mortal and corruptible to the

---

[1] Dodd, pp. 230–8.

[2] *New Testament Studies* 1, pp. 210–18, a paper entitled 'The Lamb of God'.

[3] E.g., J. Jeremias, *Eucharistic Words of Jesus*, 1955, pp. 56 f.

[4] 'Early Christian interpretation of the Passover', *Expository Times* 38 (1926–7), pp. 88 ff. and 233.

immortal and incorruptible'; again in another passage: 'a passing over from the passions to the virtuous and disciplined life'. Harris suggested that John's word μεταβαίνω in 13.1 ('his hour was come that he should depart out of this world unto the Father') receives light from Philo's conception of the Passover as a διάβασις. 'The Evangelist himself' (wrote Harris) 'invites us to see that it is Passover language that he is using.' C. A. Phillips supported this[1] by a quotation from one of Bede's Homilies which connects Jehovah's *passing* through Egypt at the original Passover, the children of Israel *passing* out of Egyptian servitude, and our Lord *passing* from this world to the Father at the time of the feast. If valid, this point would give further support to those who recognize a number of Passover allusions in the Fourth Gospel and who interpret the Lamb of 1.29 in this way.

The expression 'the Lamb *of God*' still needs elucidation. Nestle in his Greek Testament gives a marginal reference to Gen. 22.13; but 22.8, as in RVm, is more apposite, 'God will provide himself the lamb.' This may not seem very convincing at first, but it should be taken in association with other reflections of Gen. 22, the story of the offering of Isaac. Without going back on what has been said above, we may briefly explore the possibility that the incident of Genesis is reflected in John.

The early Fathers sometimes connected together (*a*) the brazen serpent, (*b*) the outstretched hands of Moses, and (*c*) the offering of Isaac, as prefiguring the Crucifixion. (Cf. Tertullian, *Answer to the Jews* 10; they are also all three in Barnabas—the offering of Isaac in 7; the outstretched hands of Moses [Ex. 17] and the brazen serpent [Num. 21] in 12.) It would therefore be of particular interest if it could be shown that all three are already present in John. We have previously considered (*a*) and (*b*) in chapters IV and V. That Gen. 22 was associated with the Cross at an early date is shown by Rom. 8.32, 'he that spared not his own son', where the verb is the same as in the LXX of Gen. 22.12, 'thou hast not withheld thy son, thine only son' (in both cases φείδομαι). It should be noticed, too, that it is in the Fourth Gospel that Jesus carries the Cross for himself (19.17): 'And he went out,

---

[1] In a note appended to the second of Harris's two contributions; see previous footnote.

bearing the cross for himself'; nothing is said of Simon of Cyrene. Barrett in his comment on 19.17 after referring to the patristic Isaac typology, adds:

it seems not impossible that John also may have had in mind some such typology, and conformed the narrative to it. This connection is perhaps reinforced by the fact that the comment on Gen. 22.6 in Gen. R. 56.4 is '. . . as one bears the cross on his shoulder'.[1] On the other hand, if John had intended this Old Testament allusion he might have been expected to make his meaning clearer.

The doubt expressed in the last sentence could be countered by remembering how very allusive John is, a master of understatement and veiled references.

Riesenfeld and others have attempted to show that the Jews in the pre-Christian period had a doctrine of expiation connected with the offering of Isaac and that this influenced the redemptive teaching of St Paul; this, however, is difficult to establish. At the same time it is of deep interest to note that the Jerusalem Targum on Gen. 22 says:

And now I pray for mercies before Thee, O Lord God, that when the children of Isaac offer in the hour of need the binding of Isaac their father, Thou mayest remember on their behalf, and remit and forgive their sins, and deliver them out of all need.

The Targum also states that when Abraham offered his son, the glory of the Shekinah of the Lord was revealed unto him.

In his commentary on Hebrews (p. 369) Westcott maintains that John 8.56 ('Abraham rejoiced to see my day') should be interpreted in the light of the tradition reflected in Heb. 11.17–19; the latter passage appears to speak of the Isaac incident in terms of death and resurrection.

It should be borne in mind that in Rabbinic teaching the story of Abraham offering Isaac, known technically as the Akeda (from the verb 'to bind' used in Gen. 22.9) held an important place. Again and again we find references to a plea that God would

---

[1] On the patristic treatment of Isaac as a type of Christ, see Daniélou, *Sacramentum Futuri*, pp. 97 ff. It should be mentioned that the words from the Genesis Midrash concerning the carrying of the cross strictly refer to Abraham, though it may well be that a reference to Isaac has dropped out at this point; cf. Israel Levi in the article mentioned below.

'remember the sacrifice of Isaac and pardon their faults'.[1] The Midrash Leviticus R. connects the Akeda with the lamb of the morning and evening sacrifice, and affirms that whenever the Israelites offer the daily sacrifice on the altar God remembers the sacrifice of Isaac. Elsewhere the Akeda is related to the Passover; thus Mekhilta 8a, 'When I see the blood of the paschal lamb . . . I will remember the blood of the Akeda.' This passage seems to assume that the slaying of Isaac actually took place; a prayer in the Talmud asks 'that God may remember for our sake the ashes of Isaac' (Taanith 16a).

All this tends to support the view that one of the strands which enter into the profound title 'the Lamb of God' comes from Genesis 22. There is warrant for Westcott's note on John 1.29 in which, after referring to Isa. 53, the Passover and the daily offering, he says:

Christ is the Lamb of God, that is, the Lamb which God Himself furnishes for sacrifice (Gen. 22.8), while the accessory notions of 'fitness for', 'belonging to', are also necessarily included in the genitive.[2]

Some authorities trace a further reference to the Isaac story in John 3.16 ('he gave his only begotten son'). Westcott writes that 'there is an obvious reference to Gen. 22.2.'[3] Bernard and Barrett regard this as a possibility.

[1] Cf. I. Levi, 'Le Sacrifice d'Isaac et la mort de Jésus', *Revue des études iuives* 64 (1912), pp. 161–84. Also H. Riesenfeld, *Jésus Transfiguré*, pp. 86–95.

[2] Cf. A. Richardson, *Introduction to the Theology of the New Testament*, pp. 228 f.

[3] Cf. F. M. Braun, *New Testament Studies* 4 (1957), p. 122, in the course of an article, 'La "lettre de Barnabé" et l'Evangile de Saint Jean', pp. 119 ff.

The word μονογενής is used of Isaac in Heb. 11.17. In Gen. 22 the LXX has ἀγαπητός and Aquila μονογενής.

XV

SUBSIDIARY POINTS

IT would be possible to find a number of other matters of comparison between Christ and Moses, but whether they were consciously in the mind of the Evangelist is not certain. The following, however, appear to be worthy of consideration.

The murmuring and attempted stoning

The word 'murmur' is used more frequently in John than in the other Gospels, and it is of interest that it is a 'wilderness word'. Rengstorf[1] has called attention to the remarkable fact that the Hebrew word *lun*, in respect of the connotation 'murmur' (for the word has other meanings), is confined to Ex. 15–17 and Num. 14–17, with the exception of one other passage, Joshua 9.18. The Exodus chapters are among those we have turned to repeatedly for they deal with the deliverance at the Red Sea, the manna and the rock.

The Greek word for 'murmur' does not occur in Mark; it is found once in Matthew, in the parable of the labourers in the vineyard (20.11), and once in Luke in regard to the Pharisees and Scribes who criticized our Lord's fellowship with sinners (5.30).[2] But in John it occurs four times: 6.41, 43, 61; 7.32. These two chapters, as we know from our earlier consideration of them, are specially relevant to the wilderness conception. The noun also is found in John 7.12. The only other occurrence of the verb in the New Testament is in I Cor. 10.10 in a context which is explicitly on the wilderness theme.

Putting the evidence of I Corinthians and John together we can say that the rebellious mood of Israel in the wilderness period has its counterpart in the attitude of the Jews of our Lord's time; and that, moreover, Christians are warned of the danger of falling into the same snare. (Cf. John 6.61, where it is the disciples who

[1] γογγύζω, *TWNT* I, p. 730.
[2] A compound form appears in Luke 15.2; 19.7.

are murmuring.) Like the Israelites of old, Christians had been delivered from bondage, given a divine supply of food and drink (I Cor. 10.3–4); but they are not yet in the land of promise; their present experience is a time of testing wherein they must not tempt God (10.9), 'neither murmur ye, as some of them murmured, and perished at the hands of the destroyer' (verse 10). This kind of exhortation is prominent in Hebrews also, particularly in connexion with Ps. 95, a psalm concerning the 'forty years' in the wilderness.

On the murmuring of John 6, Hoskyns writes: 'The murmuring of the Jews corresponds with the murmuring of their fathers in the desert' (p. 295).[1]

Murmuring and *stoning* are found together in Ex. 17 and in Num. 14. It is only in John that the Jews are described as wishing to stone Jesus; this is referred to four times: 10.31, 32, 33; 11.8. This could possibly be connected with the threat of the Israelites to stone Moses; cf. Ex. 17.4, 'they be almost ready to stone me'— the words of Moses. Another passage to consider is Num. 14.10: 'But all the congregation bade stone them (i.e. Joshua and Caleb) with stones.'

Origen, writing on Matt. 10.18, speaks of the repeated design to stone Moses.[2] While the Old Testament hardly bears out this exaggerated statement, it does show how the Israelites failed to recognize their deliverer, a fact often dwelt upon in Jewish writings. With this may be linked Stephen's words in Acts 7.25: 'He (Moses) supposed that his brethren understood how that God by his hand was giving them deliverance; but they understood not.' See verse 39 also, 'To whom our fathers would not be obedient, but thrust him from them.'

Messiah's concealment

It is particularly in John 6 and 7 that certain actions of Moses are looked for in one suspected of being the Messiah. Are there any other features of the second Moses conception in this context? It was thought that as Moses hid himself after a preliminary manifestation and then re-emerged from his obscure hiding-place, so Messiah would for a period be in concealment after his first

---

[1] Cf. Barrett on John 6.41.
[2] *TWNT* IV, p. 867, footnote 183.

appearance. According to Ruth R. (on Ruth 2.14), Rabbi Berekiah[1] said, 'As the first deliverer, so the last deliverer. As the first deliverer was revealed, then hidden and afterwards appeared again, so will it also be with the last deliverer.' There are a number of Rabbinic statements to the same effect. The same feature may be traced in one or two of the apocalypses included in A. Wünsche's *Kleine Midraschim*.

Now, it may be a coincidence or it may be more, that in John and John alone we find Jesus 'hiding' himself; the verb κρύπτω and the adjective κρυπτός are not used of Jesus in the other Gospels. At the beginning of John 7 (i.e. between the two clearly 'Mosaic' examples of the bread and the living water) the brethren of Jesus say to him, 'No man doeth anything in secret, and he himself seeketh to be known openly. If thou doest these things, manifest thyself to the world' (7.4). Then in verse 10 Jesus goes up to the feast 'not publicly, but as it were in secret'.[2] In 8.59 and 12.36 it is declared that Jesus 'hid himself'. It should be noticed that a preliminary manifestation has been mentioned in the first chapter (cf. 1.31, 'that he should be made manifest to Israel'; and 2.11).

One Jewish source[3] says that the people of Israel do not at first believe in the Messiah; he hides himself for a time and then reappears.

With this kind of tradition which is so often associated with the Moses parallelism[4] we may compare John 12.36, which is of particular importance as it comes in a statement summarizing the ministry of Jesus and its results. In John there are alternate manifestations and concealments; and the upshot is that Jesus after being manifested to Israel withdraws into hiding and finally makes himself manifest to his disciples.

The Messianic secret in the Fourth Gospel is a somewhat

[1] Berekiah's date is about AD 340 according to S.B. 2, pp. 284 f., where a number of parallels are given; the statement evidently rests upon earlier authority and among those associated with it is a Rabbi of the previous century.

[2] On John 7 and 8, see Dodd p. 348, who from a different point of view discusses Jesus' concealment; cf. also pp. 351 f. and 89.

[3] 'The Mysteries of Simeon', Wünsche, *op. cit.* 3 (1909), p. 146 ff. This is not the only apocalypse in which the Messiah first meets with unbelief.

[4] Cf. J. Klausner, *The Messianic Idea in Israel*, 1956, p. 17, footnote 16.

complicated problem.[1] But is it possible that the Moses tradition supplied one strand?

Moses as Paraclete and Intercessor

The word 'Paraclete' should be approached from the Jewish background; and it is at least interesting if nothing more that among the advocates of Israel the Holy Spirit and Moses were included (cf. *TWNT* V, p. 809). Points of contact between our Lord's high-priestly prayer and the prayer of Moses in Deut. 32–33 have been referred to in chapter x; more strictly Deut. 32 gives the song of Moses, and Deut. 33 the blessing. It is important to notice that the actual word 'Paraclete' was transliterated into Hebrew characters (*peraqlet* or *peraqlit*, from παράκλητος), and while it was used (like συνήγορος, transliterated in a similar way) in a number of connexions, at least one passage describes Moses with the exact term 'Paraclete' (Ex. R. 18.3, on Ex. 12.29). While other terms were usually employed, Moses was regarded as an outstanding intercessor for Israel.[2]

Philo uses a number of terms (though not Paraclete) in his description of Moses as advocate; thus in a passage dealing with the sin of the golden calf he writes:

Struck with dismay, and compelled to believe the incredible tale, he yet took the part of mediator and reconciler and did not hurry away at once, but first made prayers and supplications, begging that their sins might be forgiven. Then, when this protector and intercessor had softened the wrath of the Ruler, he wended his way back in mingled joy and dejection. He rejoiced that God accepted his prayers, yet was ready to burst with the dejection and heaviness that filled him at the transgression of the multitude (*Moses* II.166).

The actual description of our Lord as Paraclete occurs only in I John 2.1; but the prayer of John 17 shows him acting as Paraclete, advocate and intercessor (cf. Heb. 7.25; Rom. 8.34). Moreover, the promise of John 14.16 that the Father would send another Paraclete implies that he himself had been a Paraclete for his disciples.

It is remarkable that the intercessory work of Moses was thought of as continuing after his death. Thus in the *Assumption*

---

[1] Cf. Barrett, pp. 59 f.
[2] Cf. D. Daube, *New Testament and Rabbinic Judaism*, pp. 11 f.

of Moses, when Moses is about to die, Joshua expresses the concern of Israel; their enemies will regard them as easy prey, for they will say that now

they have no advocate to offer prayers on their behalf to the Lord, like Moses the great messenger, who every hour, day and night had his knees fixed to the earth, praying and looking for help to Him that ruleth all the world with compassion and righteousness, reminding Him of the covenant of the fathers and propitiating the Lord with the oath (11.17).

In reply Moses assures Joshua that the intercessory work will continue after his departure from the earth, for 'The Lord hath on their behalf appointed me to pray for their sins and make intercession for them' (12.6, Charles's translation and reconstruction).

The Samaritans had a tradition that Moses would carry out a priestly ministry in the heavenly sanctuary (an idea that inevitably reminds us of the teaching of the epistle to the Hebrews); see *TWNT* IV, p. 860, note 98.

Over against the intercessor stands the accuser, ὁ κατήγορος, and this word had been transliterated into Hebrew *kategor*; sometimes the two words, *peraqlit* and *kategor*, are found in the same passage (Aboth 4.13). It is significant that in John 5.45 Moses (whom the Jews regarded as their advocate) is described as their Accuser, ὁ κατηγορῶν: 'There is one that accuseth you, even Moses, on whom ye have set your hope.'

XVI

THE APOCALYPSE AND THE FOURTH GOSPEL

IT is well known that a number of terms are common to the book of Revelation and St John's Gospel and in some cases peculiar to them, e.g. the word 'Logos' as a description of Jesus Christ. This matter has, of course, an important bearing on the question of authorship, a matter in which we are not immediately interested. It is, however, of some significance that what we may call wilderness terms are to be found in this group of common words, and the interesting fact emerges that features which Revelation places in the future are in the Gospel associated with present experience. This agrees with their respective attitudes to eschatology.

Look, for instance, at the word *tabernacle*. It was a Jewish eschatological hope that in the end time God would again tabernacle with his people.[1] This is expressed, still as a hope for the future, in Rev. 21.3, 'Behold, the tabernacle of God is with men.' The reference is to a time after the first heaven and the first earth have passed away (21.1). In the Gospel, however, we find in the opening chapter the present fulfilment of this hope; the Logos, who was in the beginning with God and was God, at length 'became flesh and tabernacled among us'. Moreover, as we have noticed in earlier chapters, the realities symbolized in the Feast of Tabernacles are already present in Christ (John 7 and 8).

Again, as the Seer unveils the future he promises abundance of *water and light*. These, too, were features of the Jewish hope. Whenever Zech. 14 was read at Sukkah, it was taken as pointing forward to the end time when the promise would be fulfilled that there would be light, even at evening time (14.7), and that living waters would go out from Jerusalem (14.8). So in Rev. 21–22, in the time of the new heaven and earth, there is to be light:

[1] Cf. G. H. Boobyer, *St Mark and the Transfiguration Story*, pp. 76 ff.

And the city hath no need of the sun, neither of the moon, to shine upon it: for the glory of God did lighten it, and the lamp thereof is the Lamb. And the nations shall walk amidst the light thereof (21.23 f.).

The following chapter begins with 'a river of water of life, bright as crystal, proceeding out of the throne of God and the Lamb' (22.1). Now in the Gospel the same features of light and water are prominent, but they are present realities; see especially 8.12 and 7.37–39. In Revelation the river flowing from beneath the throne is conceived in a literal fashion and is no doubt to be considered as an actual river. But in the Gospel, the rivers of 7.38 are explicitly identified with the Holy Spirit (39). It is the same with a number of the factors mentioned in the present chapter. The difference between John and Revelation is not only one of time; features which in the latter are regarded in a more or less literal fashion are in the Gospel reinterpreted.

Again, the return of the *manna* was a feature of Jewish eschatological expectation. And accordingly in Rev. 2.17 the promise to him that overcometh is: 'To him will I give of the hidden manna.' But in the Gospel the fulfilment is a matter of present experience, for the Bread of life is the antitype of the wilderness 'bread from heaven' and is offered to all who come in faith (John 6).

The word for *palms* in John 12.13 and Rev. 7.9 is peculiar to these two passages. The ritual of the Feast of Tabernacles is suggested by this term and the 'branches of palm trees' mentioned in connexion with this feast in Lev. 23.40.[1] The fact that of the Evangelists John alone mentions this is in itself significant in the light of the Tabernacles associations already noticed in several places in this Gospel. The time indicated in John 12 is, of course, the Passover season (12.1), but the spontaneous action of the people connects with the familiar usage of Sukkah. It may also be noted that the ritual of the feast of Dedication was in part based on the usages of Sukkah; cf. II Macc. 10.6 f.:

And they kept eight days with gladness, as in the feast of the tabernacles . . . they bare branches and fair boughs and palms also, and

---

[1] 'If we examine Revelation 7 there are striking indications that the apocalyptist has the Feast of Tabernacles in mind. The palms of verse 9 are not perhaps conclusive. But when combined with phrases of the Hallel there is little doubt left' (I. Abrahams, *Studies in Pharisaism and the Gospels* II, p. 54). Cf. H. Riesenfeld, *Jésus Transfiguré*, p. 278.

sang psalms unto him that had given them good success in cleansing his place.

Burkitt thought that for John this incident had the value and meaning of a new dedication.[1] In that case the various links we have traced could suggest that three feasts were in a sense gathered up in the Triumphal Entry: Passover, Tabernacles[2] and Dedication.

In the book of Revelation the palms appear to be connected with the end time; the great multitude 'standing before the throne and before the Lamb' with palms in their hands are identified as those who have come out of the great tribulation (7.14), evidently the final tribulation. Once again an eschatological feature of Revelation is in the Gospel placed in the life of Jesus.

All these examples point in the same direction. They belong to what is known as realized eschatology. Features connected with the last times, and retained in that futuristic position by the book of Revelation, find in John their setting in the life of Jesus. We have been dealing so far with certain points which have Exodus and wilderness associations. If we widened the subject, much more material could be referred to here.

Three features of eschatological expectation which repeatedly figured in Jewish writings were (*a*) judgment, (*b*) victory over evil powers, and (*c*) the gathering of the elect or the twelve tribes. These are all found in Revelation and are still regarded as future events. But in John they are all associated with the Cross of Christ, and all in one passage (12.31 f.): 'Now is (*a*) the judgment of this world, (*b*) now shall the prince of this world be cast out; (*c*) and I if I be lifted up will draw all men unto myself.' For the Cross as the rallying-point see also 11.5, f.: '. . . he prophesied that Jesus should die for the nation; and not for the nation only, but that he might gather together into one the children of God that are scattered abroad.'

In an earlier chapter reference was made to the importance of 'looking' and 'seeing' in John, and to the words of 19.37, 'They shall look on him whom they pierced.' This same passage of Zechariah (12.10) is reflected in Rev. 1.7 and given a purely

---

[1] *Journal of Theological Studies* 17 (O.S.) (1916), pp. 139–49.

[2] T. W. Manson thought the Triumphal Entry actually took place at the Feast of Tabernacles; *Bulletin of John Rylands Library* 33 (1950–1), pp. 271–82.

future interpretation: 'Behold, he cometh with the clouds; and every eye shall see him, and they which pierced him; and all the tribes of the earth shall mourn over him' (cf. Matt. 24.30).

Again the Antichrist is future in Revelation as in other parts of the New Testament; but in John 'the son of perdition' is represented by Judas; see John 17.12, where the same phrase is used as in II Thess. 2.3.[1]

It is thus clear that the treatment of wilderness features in the Gospel and the Apocalypse is completely in line with their respective attitudes to eschatology in general. The Gospel, of course, retains the ultimate hope of 'the last day', and such references should not be regarded as interpolations; but the whole emphasis is upon what Christ has already brought within the reach of men, the fulfilment already achieved. In the book of Revelation the emphasis is on the future and on 'the things which must shortly come to pass'. This is one of several factors which make it difficult to believe in a common authorship. At the same time the use of the same imagery and the coincidences in vocabulary are notable and bear witness to a common background.

In Rev. 15.3 the martyrs standing by the glassy sea with their harps sing the song of Moses the servant of God, and the song of the Lamb. In a sense the whole of the Fourth Gospel is a singing of these two songs and a celebration of their essential unity.

It is often pointed out that in the New Testament generally the eschatological standpoint is that the expected events of the end of time have been partly fulfilled and partly still lie in the future; this has been described as eschatology realizing itself, or eschatology in process of fulfilment. In one way both John and the Apocalypse conform to this pattern. But whereas in John the main emphasis is upon the present, the life of the New Age being already available in Christ, in the Apocalypse the emphasis is mainly upon the future. The Gospel certainly retains the note of anticipation, and the Revelation is not blind to present fulfilments. But different foci of the ellipse characterize the two writings.

The imagery of Israel's desert years could be used to illustrate the general eschatological outlook of the New Testament to which

---

[1] Cf. the comments on John 17.12 of R. H. Lightfoot and C. K. Barrett.

we have just referred. In one sense the great deliverance was an event of the past; they had been rescued from Egypt and brought out of the land of bondage. Already they celebrated in song a realized redemption, for the Lord had triumphed gloriously. But at the same time they were not yet in the promised land; the full fruition was still to come. Here is to be found the tension between fulfilment and hope. If they looked back to the crossing of the Red Sea, they exulted in a divine intervention which had already taken place; but if they looked wistfully towards the crossing of Jordan, they were aware that they were still outside the promised land. God had brought them out, but he had not yet brought them in. Thus the wilderness years provide a remarkable illustration of the situation of the Christian Church today. She looks back to the great redeeming acts of God and rejoices in the blessings they have brought to her; at the same time she earnestly looks forward to the glory which shall be revealed and to the entrance into the eternal Kingdom.

INDEX OF NAMES

Abbott, E. A., 35, 53, 73
Abrahams, I., 27, 50, 107
Alford, H., 58
Ambrose, 63
Aphraates, 53
Augustine, 40, 89

Bacon, B. W., 71
Barnabas, Epistle of, 40 ff., 100
Barrett, C. K., 12 *et passim*
Bate, H. N., 42
Bauer, W., 50
Bede, 98
Bentzen, A., 18, 55, 74
Bernard, J. H., 12, 46, 100
Billerbeck, P., 12 f. *et passim*
Bloch, R., 96
Boismard, M. E., 51, 53, 55
Boobyer, G. H., 27, 69, 106
Bornhäuser, H., 49, 62, 72
Bowman, J., 20
Braun, F. M., 100
Brevint, D., 52
Bultmann, R., 29, 50, 88
Burkitt, F. C., 108

Cassian, Bishop, 44, 85
Charlier, J. P., 39
Chavasse, C., 19, 41
Cullmann, O., 35, 39, 51
Cyprian, 40, 51 ff.

Danby, H., 13 *et passim*
Daniélou, J., 17, 53, 63, 99
Daube, D., 12, 84, 104
Davies, W. D., 68, 93
Delitzsch, Franz, 18, 36, 41, 65, 97
Dodd, C. H., 13 *et passim*
Doeve, J. W., 12, 59
Driver, S. R., 77

Ephrem, 53
Eusebius, 23, 51, 70, 85

Finch, R. G., 49
Fischer, J., 16
Fortunatus, 37
Frazer, J. G., 62

Gelasius, 77
Gfrörer, A. F., 24, 46
Ginsburg, C. D., 36, 65, 76
Ginzberg, L., 43, 95
Godet, F., 58, 61
Greenup, A. W., 58
Gregory of Nyssa, 53
Guilding, A., 50, 81
Gutbrod, W., 92, 94

Hardman, O., 10
Harris, J. R., 65, 87, 97
Heidel, W. A., 55
Henry, M., 37, 52, 58
Hochman, J., 60
Hooker, M., 19
Horovitz, H. G., 83
Hoskyns, E., 13, 40, 48 f., 51, 86, 102

Ignatius, 37
Irenaeus, 40

Jastrow, M., 39
Jeremias, J., 20, 50, 72, 97
Josephus, 18, 32
Justin, 38, 40, 42 f.

Kilpatrick, G. D., 50
King, E. G., 51, 72
Kittel, G., 87
Klausner, J., 16, 93, 103

Lactantius, 37
Lagrange, M.-J., 12 f. *et passim*
Lampe, G. W. H., 63
Levi, I., 99 f.
Levner, I. B., 96
Lightfoot, J., 54, 58
Lightfoot, J. B., 28 f., 37, 45 f., 90
Lightfoot, R. H., 13, 72, 109
Lindars, B., 35
Lods, A., 55
Loisy, A., 13, 48, 50 f., 72

Manson, T. W., 42, 68, 108
Marsh, J., 13
Mauser, U., 17
Meyer, F. B., 10, 68, 82
Meyer, R., 46
Moody, D. L., 10
Moule, H. C. G., 84
Mowinckel, S., 18
Munck, J., 74

Neale, J. M., 15
Nestle, E., 98
Newton, E., 33

Odeberg, H., 92
Oesterley, W. O. E., 75
Origen, 10, 53, 102

Phillips, C. A., 98
Phillips, G. L., 35
Philo, 25, 31, 43, 70, 95 ff., 104

Ramsey, A. M., 68, 70
Rengstorf, K. H., 101
Richardson, A., 100
Riesenfeld, H., 49, 62, 99 f., 107
Robinson, J. A. T., 28

Salkinson, I., 36, 65, 76
Selwyn, E. C., 52
Singer, S., 39
Smothers, E. R., 30
Stillingfleet, E., 23
Strack, H. L., 12 f. *et passim*
Strauss, D. F., 71

Taylor, V., 71
Teeple, H. M., 92
Tertullian, 98
Tintoretto, 33
Toplady, A. M., 52
Trench, R. C., 26

Wagenseil, J. C., 70
Wesley, C., 9 f., 52, 56
Westcott, B. F., 10 f. *et passim*
Wiebe, W., 17
Williams, W., 64
Wilpert, J., 22
Woollcombe, K. J., 63
Wordsworth, C., 58, 67
Wünsche, A., 82, 103

Zeno of Verona, 63

INDEX OF REFERENCES

Genesis
2.7 84
22 98 ff.
24 57

Exodus
3.12–15 81
4.8 78 f.
4.19 21
6.3 77
7.19 f. 26
12 97
13 49
14.19 17
14.31 78
15 73
15–17 101 f.
17 Ch. V, 55 ff., 98
23.30 75
24 71
24.8 15
24.18 22
25.8 65
25.9, 40 80
26.30 80
27.8 80
29.4 82
33.7–11 66
33.18 77
33.20 25
34.6 f. 97
34.29 ff. 69 ff.

Leviticus
16.4 82
23.40 ff. 48, 50, 66, 107
26.11 f. 66, 76

Numbers
8.4 80
12.7 f. 25
14–17 101 f.
14.11 81
16.28 79
20 49, 55 ff.
21 Ch. IV, 98
21.17 f. 55 f., 59
27.15–23 80 ff., 95

Deuteronomy
1.3, 21, 29 74 f.
4.37 75
5.10 75
6.13, 16 76
7.6 f., 9, 18 75
8.3 76
8.14 ff. 33
9.9 22
9.11 81
10.4 81
10.15 75
11.1, 22 75 f.
13.3 f. 75
14.2 75
16.18 81
17.6 78
18.15 ff. 20 ff., 27, 30 ff., 80
18.21 21
19.9, 15 75 f.
21.5 75
30.11 93
30.16, 20 75 f.
31.7 f. 74 f., 83
32 f. Ch. X
33.5 31
34.9 83 ff.
34.10 25

Joshua
22.5 76
23.8–11 76

I Kings
8.10 66

Nehemiah
9.12–15 48, 62

Psalms
77.20 95
78.15–27 48, 54
80.8 ff. 91
95 101
105.39–41 48, 62

Proverbs
3.19 87
6.23 86
8 86 f.
25.21 86

Ecclesiastes
12.11 96

Isaiah
4.5 f. 17, 64, 67
5.26 36 f.
10.24–26 16
11.12 36
11.15 f. 16
13.2 36
18.3 36
40–55 16–18
48.21 17, 52
53 100
62.10 36
63.11 15, 22, 95
65.2 42, 44

Jeremiah		Luke		John	
2.21	91	15.3–7	96	7.24	81
31.31 ff.	17	16.11	90	7.37 ff.	Ch. VII, 72, 106 f.
		22.37	19		
Ezekiel		23.33	41	7.40 f.	27 ff.
20.33 ff.	16			7.42	31
47	58	John		7.49	91
48.35	67	1.1–18	65 ff., 86 ff.	7.52	30
		1.9	64, 88, 91	7.53 ff.	60, 72, 91
Hosea		1.14	34, Ch. IX, 106	8.12	58, Ch. VIII, 72, 107
2.14	16	1.17 f.	24 ff., 70, 81, 86	8.17	92
				8.20	60
Micah		1.19–25	28 f., 71	8.28	30, 35, 80
7.15	16	1.25 ff.	27, 57, 71	8.42	80
		1.29	16, 34, 96 ff.	8.50, 54	72
Zechariah		1.31	103	8.56	99
12.10	35, 52, 108	1.36	34	8.59	103
13.1	52	1.50 f.	34 f.	9.5	91
14	49, 60, 72, 106	2.1 ff.	26, 57 f., 71, 88, 103	9.7–15	57, 89
				9.28 f.	91
Malachi		3.5	57	10	81, 85, 96
4.5	27	3.14	Ch. IV, 43	10.3, 16	79
		3.16	100	10.25, 37	80
Matthew		3.22 ff.	57	10.27, 38	79
2.15	22	4	53 ff., 89, 91	10.28 f.	96
2.20	21 f.	4.25	20, 30, 32	10.31–33	102
4.2	22	5.2 ff.	57, 89	10.34	92
5–7	22, 92	5.19	80	11.51 f.	36, 108
17.2	70	5.30, 36, 43	80	12.13	107
19.17	75	5.35	28, 91	12.21 ff.	35, 72 f.
20.11	101	5.37	79	12.31	108
21.11	30	5.39–47	89 f.	12.32–34	35, 37, 44, 73, 108
23.2	12	5.45	105	12.36	103
24.26	18	6	Ch. VI, 90 f., 107	12.37	81
24.30	109	6–7	102 ff.	12.49 f.	30, 80
27.38	41	6.14 f.	27 ff.	13–17	Ch. X
		6.35	50	13.1 ff.	57, 82 ff., 97 f.
Mark		6.40	34 f.	13.30 ff.	72 f.
9.2 ff.	68 ff.	6.41, 43	101	13.34 f.	80, 92 f.
14.24	15	6.46	26	13.36	44
15.27	41	6.61	101	14.1 f.	83 f.
		7.3, 16, 28	80	14.9	35
Luke		7.12, 32	101	14.10	80
1.17	28	7.19–22	90–92	14.11	79
5.30	101				
7.39	30				

John

14.15	93
14.16	104
14.19	35
14.21	93
14.27	83
15.1	91
15.10	93
15.16	84 f.
15.24	80
15.25	97
15.27	84
16.16	35
17	104
17.4, 8	80
17.12	96, 109
17.22	81 ff.
17.24	35
18.1–6	71
18.9	96
18.36	31
18.37	79
19.7	92
19.17	98 f.
19.18	Ch. V
19.29	97
19.34	51 ff.
19.35	35
19.36	97
19.37	34 f.
20.8	35

John

20.22	84 f.
20.29	35
21	84 f.
21.18 f.	42, 44

Acts

3.22	21
7.25	102
7.37	21
7.39	102
10.37	28
13.24	28
21.38	18

Romans

8.32	98
8.34	104
10.21	42

I Corinthians

1.22–25	38, 87
5.7 f.	15, 97
10.1 ff.	15, 48 ff., 101 f.

II Corinthians

3	26, 69 f., 92
4.1–6	69
5.1	68
6.16	76

Colossians

1.15–20	87
2.17	90

I Thessalonians

1.9	90

II Thessalonians

2.3	109

Hebrews

1.3	87
3.1–6	25, 69
4	9
7.25	104
8	80
10.22	82
11.17–19	99
13.20	15, 22, 95

I Peter

1.18 f.	15, 97

I John

2.1	104

Revelation

1.7	108
2.17	46, 107
7.9, 14	107 f.
11	27, 69
15.3	96, 109
21–22	72, 106 f.